a·non·y·pon·y·mous

Etienne de SILHOUETTE

a·non·y·pon·y·mous

THE FORGOTTEN PEOPLE BEHIND EVERYDAY WORDS

John Bemelmans Marciano

NEW YORK   BERLIN   LONDON

Published by Bloomsbury USA, New York

All papers used by Bloomsbury USA are natural, recyclable products made
from wood grown in well-managed forests. The manufacturing processes
conform to the environmental regulations of the country of origin.

LIBRARY OF CONGRESS CONTROL NUMBER: 2009928110

ISBN 978-1-59691-653-1

First U.S. Edition 2009

3   5   7   9   10   8   6   4   2

Interior design by Sara E. Stemen

Printed in the United States of America by Worldcolor Fairfield

For my father

INTRODUCTION

The smiling gent you see on the front cover is John Montagu, the fourth Earl of Sandwich. If he's grinning it might be because he's famous, saved from oblivion by the way he liked to snack, with a slab of salt beef stuffed between two pieces of toast. Or maybe it's because he's just won big. The earl was such a degenerate gambler that he once stayed at the wagering tables twenty-four hours straight, which is why he invented the sandwich in the first place—so he wouldn't have to get up.

The Earl of Sandwich is famous for being the man behind a word that most people never thought was named after anyone, a man both anonymous and eponymous or, to coin a term, anonyponymous.

As a word, *eponymous* is a bit anonymous itself. Its moment in the sun came with the release of REM's album *Eponymous*, a subtle dig at musicians who name records after themselves, such as Peter Gabriel, whose first four albums are all entitled *Peter Gabriel*. In short, an eponym is anything that's ever been named after anybody. The title of an autobiography, the name of a legal firm, Mercedes-Benz, Washington State—anything.

But eponymy doesn't necessarily involve the conscious act of naming. An eponym can also be a word that explodes into the language because of who a person is or what he or she did, often to that person's dismay. For how this happens, here's a firsthand account by Dr. Frasier Crane, as told to Sam Malone in an episode of *Cheers*:

> *Frasier, explaining being left at the altar*: The story of my humiliation spread like wildfire through the university, and then to the entire Italian countryside. Everyone knew about it, everyone knew about my shame.
>
> *Sam*: Naw—you must have been imagining that.
>
> *Frasier*: Oh, was I? Do you know that in soccer, when a player kicks at the ball, misses, and falls down, it's now called a Frasier?
>
> *Sam*: That could be a coincidence.
>
> *Frasier*: If he's knocked cold, it's called a Frasier Crane.

Names often get used in this type of descriptive shorthand, like with, "That kid's a real Einstein," or, "He pulled a Bernie Madoff." But a name only crosses into true word-hood once it is no longer used as a reference. When we speak of hectoring wives and philandering husbands, it is without a picture of valiant Hector or lover-boy Philander popping into our minds, the way a bespectacled Viennese man with a pipe does when we say "Freudian slip." To be considered anonyponymous, a word must pass the Viennese pipe test.

So what are the other criteria? First, that the word be an eponym, the determining of which can present more of a challenge than you might think. Like most New Yorkers, I long believed the Outerbridge Crossing got its name from being the bridge farthest from downtown, and was shocked to learn that it instead honored Eugenius Harvey Outerbridge. Outerbridge is an example of the perfectly well-suited name, or aptronym, and whether a person is eponym or aptronym can be a chicken-or-the-egg propo-sition. Sometimes a famous name mirrors an existing term and reinforces it, as might have happened with Philadelphia whiskey maker E. G. Booz. There also lurks the possibility of nominative determinism, when someone's name influences what they become—perhaps what drove Learned Hand to become one of the most influential justices in U.S. history.

The other half of the equation—the anonymous part—cannot be decided absolutely, as everyone's knowl-edge is different. Most readers will know some of the char-acters in the following pages; the hope is that all the figures will be a surprise for the majority of readers. My editor thought Guy Fawkes had become too familiar due to the *V for Vendetta* mask, but I had never seen the movie. I since have, but not everyone has made the same mistake. Age is a big dividing line, and what is an eponym to one generation will be an anonyponym for the next. On the brink is a word like *hoover*, gaining traction as a verb meaning to suck something up. Its vibrant onomatopoeic quality almost assures its continued use among those ignorant of its origins, but I can never get out of my mind that it's the name of a vacuum manufacturer, so it failed the Viennese pipe test.

Not everyone who qualifies under the rules made it into the book, of course. In general, I preferred naturally occurring, Frasier Crane–type eponyms, so mythological figures and fictional characters were preferred to inventors and scientists: hence the absence of such delightful names as Henry J. Heimlich (maneuver), Robert Wilhelm Bunsen (burner), and Fernand Lamaze (class). Finally, there were those people who didn't qualify but I included anyway, such as the Marquis de Sade (because how could I leave out the Marquis de Sade?).

One person I didn't feel comfortable bending the rules for was our friend the Earl of Sandwich, who has become famous for his very obscurity. I do, however, want to propose the earl as patron saint of the anonyponymous. His example shows that there is hope for the forgotten figures populating the following pages, that perhaps their lives can also be pulled out of the shadows of history for the wider world to recognize. It's fair to ask, however, why should they be?

All words are abstractions. But words also have histories, and by unwinding them, we gain access to the hidden richness of our language. The absolute origins of words are for the most part unknowable; what makes eponyms extraordinary is that we can point to the moment of their birth and to the lives of the people from whom they sprang.

But why *anony*ponyms? Blame Etienne de Silhouette. When I looked up the etymology of the word *silhouette* and saw his name, I thought a virus had somehow infected my copy of the OED. It seemed like a prank, and indeed, Monsieur Silhouette and many of the other folks herein would see their peculiar fame as exactly that. In the anonyponymous, biographical history and the dictionary intersect in the realm of the ridiculous—and also of the remarkable, the delightful, and the fascinating.

I hope you enjoy these words and the people behind them as much as I have.

Muhammad ibn Musa
al-KHWARIZMI

al·go·rithm *n. A set of rules for solving a problem.*
No, the first anonyponymous person in the book is not
Al Gore.

When a word begins with *al-*, there's a good chance it
comes from Arabic. This is true with *alchemy, almanac, al-
cove, alcohol* (ironically), and *algorithm*, named for Muhammad ibn Musa al-Khwarizmi, or, as his Latin translators
called him, Algorismus.

In the early ninth century Baghdad was fast becoming the world's most important center of trade and learning, and while engaged at its illustrious House of Wisdom,
al-Khwarizmi produced his most famous work, *The Book of
Restoring and Balancing.* In it, al-Khwarizmi explained how to
solve complex mathematical equations by a method called
al-jabr, Arabic for "reunion of broken parts," which came
rendered in Latin as "algebra." (See about those *al-* words?)
On an even more basic level, al-Khwarizmi was instrumen-
tal in the spread of Arabic numerals. Not that he invented
them, nor did any Arab; the symbols originated on the Indian
subcontinent in the centuries leading up to Christ.

The set of rules laid down by al-Khwarizmi for working with these fancy Hindu number signs was so revolutionary that his name came to mean arithmetic, first in the Arab world, and then in the form *algorism* throughout the West. But this wouldn't happen until al-Khwarizmi's books were finally translated into Latin, about three hundred years after he wrote them, an indication of just how far the Christian world lagged behind the Muslim one during the intellectual deep freeze of the Middle Ages. Roman numerals—a system invented for notching sticks—didn't get replaced by Hindu-Arabic ones until the mid-1500s.

bou·gain·vil·lea *n. A kind of flowering vine.*
Louis-Antoine de Bougainville set sail in late 1766 attempting to become the first Frenchman to circumnavigate the globe. Along for the ride was botanist Philibert Commerçon and the young man he had hired as his valet for the trip, Jean Bonnefoy. Bonnefoy was both dedicated and tireless, trekking everywhere with Commerçon and turning into quite a talented botanist himself. Among the many plants they discovered was one they found in Brazil, a climbing, flowering shrub that Commerçon named in his admiral's honor.

Still, the most celebrated stop on the trip wasn't South America but the South Pacific, specifically Tahiti, first revealed to the wider world in Bougainville's later writings.

Bougainville described the island as a kind of earthly paradise peopled by noble savages uncorrupted by civilization. Uncorrupted, maybe, but not fools. When they saw Commerçon's young assistant, they immediately knew what the crew hadn't yet figured out, namely, that *he* was a *she*.

Jean Bonnefoy was in fact Jeanne Baret. Tearfully, the young woman explained to Bougainville that she'd adopted her drag persona in order to make a living after the death of her parents. Hearing all the hoopla surrounding Bougainville's trip, she approached Commerçon with an offer to serve as his valet. Despite sharing a cabin with her (unusual for a master and servant in those days), Commerçon never managed to figure out her gender. Bougainville wasn't bothered by the ruse and punished no one, but the admiral hadn't heard the real story. Commerçon had known all along about Baret—he'd apparently hired her two years before the voyage as his housekeeper, and had even placed her in his will. Were they lovers? No one knows for sure, but they certainly spent a lot of time inside that cabin together.

In any event, Bougainville's convoy arrived home to Brittany in 1769 with Jeanne Baret aboard, making her the first woman of any nationality to circumnavigate the globe.

AMESNAY OF OWERSFLAY

To describe and categorize every living thing was the main mission in life of Carolus Linnaeus, the most prolific namer in history. Living in the eighteenth century toughened Linnaeus's task, as discoveries were daily rolling in from every corner of the globe. To keep up, the brainy Swede and his fellow botanists named many of the new plants after people. To fit into Linnaeus's system of nomenclature, an *-ia* was added to honorees' surnames in a kind of scientific pig Latin. (The Swede's own real name: Karl Lineé.)

Botanists sometimes honored their patrons, as Philibert Commerçon had with Bougainville, but mostly they just honored each other. To give you some idea: Linnaeus named the zinnia after German botanist Johann Zinn and the gardenia after Scottish-American botanist Alexander Garden (an aptronym if ever there was one), plus the little-known plumeria after Charles Plumier, a French botanist who in turn honored his countrymen Michel Bégon and Pierre Magnol as well as an important German botanist of an earlier generation, Leonhart Fuchs.

Madame Hortense Lepaute, on the other hand, was not a botanist but an astronomer; she owes her floral honor to Commerçon, ever willing to help out a lady in a man's world.

A Floral Sampling

FORSYTHIA

FUCHSIA

HORTENSIA

Michel Bégon

Louis-Antoine de Bougainville

Anders Dahl

William Forsyth

Friedrich Freese

Leonhart Fuchs

Alexander Garden

Hortense Lepaute

Pierre Magnol

Joel Poinsett

Caspar Wistar

Johann Zinn

bowd·ler·ize *v. To omit or change material considered vulgar, offensive, or otherwise unseemly.*

> I acknowledge Shakespeare to be the world's greatest dramatic poet, but regret that no parent could place the uncorrected book in the hands of his daughter.
> — FROM THE PREFACE TO THE *Family Shakespeare*

Thomas Bowdler was a wealthy English gentleman who studied medicine but never practiced, preferring to devote his life to prison reform, playing chess, and providing the world with offense-free Shakespeare. The first volume of the *Family Shakespeare* saw the light of day in 1807, with editorial changes ranging from the trivial to the silly—as in replacing the exclamation "God!" with "Heavens!" (great for the old iambic pentameter) or putting "Out crimson spot!" for "Out damned spot." But some were indeed significant, as when Hamlet's beloved Ophelia dies not as a suicide but the victim of an accidental drowning.

Although the idea of changing the Bard's words seems unspeakably presumptuous today, in Bowdler's time the plays of Shakespeare had yet to acquire the status of holy works. In fact, most were already performed in altered versions, the restoration of his works not occurring until the latter half of the nineteenth century. Already in Shakespeare's own time actors and stage directors were cutting large swaths of text and tampering with scenes: It's just that, before Bowdler, they tended to play *up* the naughty bits. For this reason the most popular of Shakespeare's works was long *Richard III*; audiences just loved Colley Cibber's "blood-and-thunder" version of the play.

With the dawn of the uptight Victorian era, the *Family Shakespeare* became a bestseller and mainstay of the middle-class home, but no matter its success, Mr. Bowdler became a figure of ridicule. His critics got the final word—by coining one after him.

Ironically, though, Bowdler didn't even do his own hatchet work. Bowdler's sister was his ghost editor—in fact, the 1807 edition was her handiwork entirely. The reason her name couldn't appear on the book, it seems, is that it wasn't considered proper for a lady to come into contact with such lewd and vulgar material.

boy·cott *n. A protest effected by refusing to patronize, attend, or in any way support the existence of.*
After life as a captain in the British army, a cush job in the Irish countryside must have sounded pretty good to Charles Boycott. But he had no idea what he was signing up for when he became land agent for the County Mayo estates of Lord Erne. Things went well at first, until a bad harvest across Ireland in 1879 sowed fears of a second potato famine.

This led to the formation of the Land League, a nationalist organization that promised action against anyone who served writs of eviction against Irish tenant farmers. When Boycott started doing just that, he became the league's first target. Savvy of public opinion, the league proceeded in a nonviolent mode, directing the community to ostracize Boycott: No shop would serve him, the postman stopped delivering his mail, and even his church congregation gave him the deep freeze. The British government, outraged by Irish temerity, paid for upwards of a thousand men of the Royal Irish Constabulary to protect the fifty scabs Boycott hired to bring in Lord Erne's crops.

The potatoes were successfully harvested, albeit at a reported cost of nearly thirty times what they were worth (a poor calculus even by current U.S. farm-policy standards). Boycott left the Emerald Isle before Christmas and the following year Prime Minister William Gladstone introduced legislation that secured all of the basic rights the Land League sought, rendering the first boycott a smashing success.

brag·ga·do·cio *n. Unwarranted boasting, usually male.*
In Edmund Spenser's *The Faerie Queene* (1590–1596), Braggadocchio is a dishonorable knight who steals the horse of the Knight of Temperance: "Vaine Braggadocchio getting Guyons horse is made the scorne / Of knighthood trew."

The Faerie Queene was an epic poem greatly indebted to Italian works like *Orlando Furioso*. Because of this, and because it was an allegorical work, Spenser came up with an Italian-sounding name for his vainglorious knight based on the English word *brag*. (Spenser wasn't much into subtlety.) For some odd reason, the pseudo-Italian name Braggadocchio has taken on the pseudo-Spanish spelling *braggadocio*. In any event, the word is a purely English concoction.

car·di·gan *n. A jacketlike sweater fastened with buttons or a zipper.*

> *Theirs not to make reply,*
> *Theirs not to reason why,*
> *Theirs but to do and die:*
> *Into the valley of Death*
> *Rode the six hundred.*

Wearing their cardigan sweaters.

The Charge of the Light Brigade, immortalized in the poem by Alfred Lord Tennyson, was a big fat mistake. A miscommunicated order during the Crimean War's Battle of Balaclava (1854) led to a cavalry assault so foolhardy that the enemy Russian troops thought the onrushing Brits had to be drunk. The doomed but brave sally sparked the English imagination in a romantic period when the doomed but brave was much celebrated. (Tennyson's "Charge of the Heavy Brigade at Balaclava," about a more successful cavalry action, was far less of a hit.)

The leader of the charge managed to make it through unscathed and went home to England a hero, an unlikely outcome for James Thomas Brudenell, the seventh Earl of Cardigan. Cardigan had risen through the army via family connections and purchasing commissions; he certainly didn't do it by being an upstanding citizen or military man, having led a scandalous home life with wives and mistresses and winding up in court on numerous occasions for egregiously overreacting to the supposed transgressions of subordinates.

In one respect, however, he treated his men splendidly. Wanting his Eleventh Hussars to be the spiffiest regiment in the Queen's army, Cardigan spent an estimated ten thousand pounds a year of his personal fortune outfitting them. Reportedly, this included a knitted, button-down vest of Cardigan's own invention that he and his men wore under their battle uniforms to stave off the Crimean cold. Whether true or the fantasy of an enterprising sweater salesman, the story was widely believed, and with everyone wanting to copy the heroes of the Light Brigade the cardigan became the fashion of the day.

What would Mr. Rogers have done without them?

ce·re·al *n. 1. An edible grain, or the plant from which it comes. 2. A mass-produced breakfast food, generally served suspended in a bowl of milk.*

Though little considered nowadays, Ceres was among the more venerated Roman gods. As goddess of the crops, she was especially associated with grains and was thus the go-to deity for people looking to avert famine. *Cereal* originally referred to anything that had to do with Ceres but narrowed in meaning to "of grains" or grain itself, at least until a guy named Kellogg came along.

Dr. John Kellogg ran a peculiar sort of health spa that promoted the Sylvester Graham–inspired dietary principles of the Seventh Day Adventists (see *graham cracker*). At the Battle Creek Sanitarium patients consumed a lot of nuts but no alcohol or tobacco and exercised vigorously. They also became intimately acquainted with Dr. Kellogg's enema machine, a device that swiftly pumped gallons of water up the paying guests' bowels, followed by a half-pint chaser of yogurt, "thus planting the protective germs where they are most needed and may render most effective service." Modern research is just now coming around to certain of Kellogg's theories on intestinal flora; coupled with his balanced, high-fiber diet, the doctor might seem like a visionary. His sexual beliefs, however, made him a quack.

"Neither the plague, nor war, nor small-pox, nor similar diseases, have produced results so disastrous to humanity as the pernicious habit of onanism."

To do the widest possible good, Kellogg got into the business of manufacturing bland, masturbation-suppressing breakfast cereal. The concept of breakfast cereal had been created in 1863 when Kellogg's rival James Caleb Jackson introduced Granula to the world. Made from graham flour, Granula was like Grape-Nuts, except even worse; you had to soak the stuff overnight just to make it edible. Improving upon Jackson's idea, Kellogg invented the cereal flake and went into business with his little brother Will selling boxes of the stuff. When Will suggested putting some sugar on the cereal so people might actually want to eat it, John was horrified. More businessman than idealist, Will set off on his own in 1906 and founded the company that would become Kellogg's, and within three years was selling millions of boxes of his sweetly delicious Toasted Corn Flakes.

Disappointingly for John, breakfast cereal did little to arrest practice of the "solitary vice," and he'd cringe at the ten-billion-dollar-a-year corn-and-sugar-peddling conglomerate that he unwittingly set into motion. There may still be hope for those yogurt enemas, though.

chau·vin·ism *n. 1. Fanatical patriotism. 2. Belief in the superiority of one's own gender, again, usually male.*

Nicolas Chauvin served in both the Army of the First Republic and Napoleon's Grand Armée. He was wounded seventeen times, leaving him severely disfigured and maimed. That didn't dampen his fighting spirit, though; Chauvin remained a jingoistic patriot and die-hard supporter of Napoleon through every hardship. His loyalty paid off when the emperor personally presented Chauvin with the Saber of Honor and a pension of two hundred francs. In later, less nationalistic days, Chauvin's blind loyalty led to his becoming the butt of sarcasm in various snarky French plays.

The inability of historians to turn up any details on Chauvin's life in the public record has led to the suggestion that he is a purely mythical figure, which for poor Monsieur Chauvin would be the final indignity.

com·stock·ery *n. Fanatical desire to censor on moral grounds.*

If Thomas Bowdler was a harbinger of the prudish Victorian era, Anthony Comstock represented the age in its fullest flower. The McCarthy of the Cold War against sin, Comstock served in the Union infantry, where he objected to the incessant cursing of his fellow soldiers, then moved to New York City, where he found himself further appalled. All around this modern Gomorrah were prostitution, pornography, and explicit ads for birth control, the very existence of which Comstock believed "promoted lust."

But when you're in a new town there's no need to feel down, and Comstock found the place he could go: the YMCA. The YMCA was then still very much the Young Men's Christian Association; Comstock, already tipping off police to illegal pornography, greatly impressed its leaders, who invited him to join their Society for the Suppression of Vice.

In 1872, Mr. Comstock went to Washington. He lobbied Congress to pass what would become known as the first Comstock Law, an act that criminalized the mailing and interstate transportation of "obscene, lewd, or lascivious" material, contraceptives included. Each offense was punishable by a *minimum* of six months' hard prison labor. Furthermore, Comstock was made a special agent of the Postal Service and given the right to carry a gun and arrest people, which he did with gusto.

Anthony

COMSTOCK

This self-declared "weeder in God's garden" would go on to achieve thousands of convictions during a career that stretched into the twentieth century, for which he attracted many admirers (including a certain cereal-pioneering anti-onanist). While Comstock did do unquestionable good in prosecuting public frauds, his most attention-grabbing campaigns were those aimed at political activists and artists. In 1905, however, an artist-activist bit back when George Bernard Shaw coined a term for America's censorship movement.

"Comstockery is the world's standing joke at the expense of the United States. Europe likes to hear of such things. It confirms the deep-seated conviction of the Old World that America is a provincial place, a second-rate country-town civilization after all."

In retaliation, Comstock vowed to investigate the "Irish smut dealer" and directed police to the New York premiere of Shaw's *Mrs. Warren's Profession*, resulting in the arrest of most of those involved and shuttering the production, thereby ensuring the play's future popularity. (Shaw's biggest obscenity controversy was still to come; see *pygmalion*.)

FAHRENHEIT VS. CELSIUS

In 1714, German physicist Gabriel Fahrenheit made a scale for measuring temperature using mercury in an enclosed glass tube, creating the first modern thermometer. His system enjoyed wide popularity until a Swedish astronomer by the name of Anders Celsius proposed his Johnny-come-lately thermometer in a paper he presented to the Royal Swedish Academy of Sciences in 1742. With its simplistic 0°–100° freeze-boil metric and the appeal of a new thing, Celsius's centigrade scale caught on. In 1948, it was renamed for the man who invented it, and with the ensuing march of the metric system across the globe, Celsius knocked Fahrenheit off thermometers just about everywhere but in the United States, which, along with a few other bastions of free thought such as Myanmar, remains steadfast in refusing to accept a soulless measurement system. Mr. Fahrenheit would applaud.

(Incidentally, Celsius originally had 0° and not 100° representing the boiling point, but Carolus Linnaeus did his fellow Swede a solid by reversing the scale. In a way Linnaeus was returning a favor: For a time Anders's uncle Olof Celsius had given the botanist a place to crash when he was hard up for money.)

crap·per *n. A toilet; also, in phr. "crapper material," a book or magazine meant to be read in the bathroom, e.g., this one.*

Thomas Crapper is a man yet to receive his due. Most reputable arbiters of etymology deem urban legend the idea that he had anything to do with the word *crapper*. To be sure, the term *crap* predates Mr. Crapper. *Crappa* was a medieval Latin term meaning "chaff," from which developed many variations, all generally meaning something leftover or garbagey. Crapper as a last name similarly has agricultural roots: It is a variation on cropper.

The first usage of crap in regards to shit is recorded in 1846, too early for it to have anything to do with Thomas Crapper, who was not yet ten. Young Crapper, however, would grow up to be an early purveyor of the flush toilet. His London firm manufactured thousands of such toilets, all emphatically marked CRAPPER'S. American servicemen visiting London during the Great War thought this was the funniest damn thing they had ever seen, and, according to one theory, brought back home with them a new word.

It does seem fair to question, however, just how a plumbing-fixtures manufacturer came by so serendipitous a surname. Fate? Or was it a case of nominative determinism, in which Thomas's surname steered him into his life's work? Or did Thomas *choose* the name Crapper for professional advantage? Now that would show some serious dedication to marketing.

Thomas CRAPPER

cur·ry fa·vor *v. To kiss ass.*

Fauvel was a horse who decided it was high time to move out of the barn and into the master's house. With the assistance of Dame Fortune, his wish came true; rather than be satisfied, however, Fauvel developed a thirst for power, and powerful he became. His fame spread—an animal in such a position must have been an important lord indeed—and the most important noblemen and church grandees from all over the land came to pay homage. In the presence of the great Fauvel, they bowed down to the horse and groomed him, showing that such people will do anything, no matter how humiliating, to gain favor.

The fable of Fauvel—an allegory for the corruption of church and state—first appeared in France in the early 1300s. Authored anonymously for political reasons, the *Roman de Fauvel* followed in the tradition of beast epics such as the *Roman de Renart*, albeit satirically. As for the character of Fauvel, the fauve-colored ass or horse had long symbolized hypocrisy, assumedly not owing to the Bambi-like hue itself but to the similarity between *fauve* and another French word, *faus*—modern *faux*—from the same root as the English *false*. Lest anyone miss the point, the author provided an acrostic explanation for the name in his poem, listing among the horse's attributes F*latterie*, A*varice* (greed), V*ilenie* (guile), V*ariété* (inconstancy), E*nvie*, and L*âcheté* (cowardice). This, of course, spells Favvel, but u's and v's were used interchangeably back then so it didn't matter.

But why is it "to curry favor" and not "to groom Fauvel"? *Curry* is a defunct synonym for *groom*, though not defunct entirely, which anyone who's ever currycombed a horse will know. As for *Fauvel* becoming *favor*, well, it just made more sense that way, especially to someone unfamiliar with the story. Another example of this type of folk etymology is *bridegroom*, once *bridegome*. *Gome* originally meant *man* (it is a cognate of the Latin *homo*) but fell out of use shortly after Chaucer's day. *Groom*, before becoming horse-specific, signified a male servant of any kind, making it a perfectly apt replacement for its archaic near homonym.

Del·a·ware *n. 1. A river in the northeastern U.S. 2. A Native American tribe. 3. A small, insignificant U.S. state.*

Baron Thomas West De La Warre, freshly appointed governor of the Jamestown colony, landed on the Virginia coast in 1610 to find that the settlers there had had enough of this New World crap and were heading home to England. De La Warre ordered their ship turned around, assuring them that under his regime the settlers wouldn't have so much to worry about. The local Powhatan tribe, however, would. The chief of the Powhatans had gone to war against the settlers (his daughter Pocahontas's fondness for them be damned), an act the new governor for life set about punishing by raiding Native American villages, burning down houses and crops, stealing food, and kidnapping children. These were Irish tactics, skills De La Warre had honed putting down revolts on the Emerald Isle. They soon just became American tactics, and the process of freeing the land of its home braves was underway.

die·sel *n. 1. A type of fuel. 2. An engine designed to run on said fuel. 3. A rusting, homely, hard-to-start car from the 1970s.*

For those of you who blame 9/11 on George Bush and believe the Kennedy assassination was orchestrated by the military-industrial complex, I present to you Rudolf Diesel.

In 1897, Diesel unveiled a 25-horsepower engine revolutionary in its simplicity and superior efficiency. Diesel engines soon were everywhere, and Rudolf became wealthy off the royalties. Although he had investigated fuel sources such as ammonia steam, coal dust, and vegetable oil, Diesel settled on liquid petroleum to power his creation. However, at the 1900 World's Fair in Paris a diesel engine was run using peanut oil, a demonstration commissioned by the French, who were lacking in oil fields but had peanuts in abundance. Nothing came of the experiment, but in 1912 Diesel reflected back on the event, drawing conclusions that sound shockingly modern.

The fact that fat oils from vegetable sources can be used may seem insignificant today, but such oils ... make it certain that motor-power can still be produced from the heat of the sun, which is always available for agricultural purposes, even when all our natural stores of solid and liquid fuels are exhausted.

A year later, Diesel was dead. Was it an accident, suicide, or assassination? Here are the facts:

On September 29, 1913, Diesel boarded an overnight boat from Antwerp to London and was last seen going on deck around ten P.M. When attendants came to his cabin at six fifteen the next morning to wake him, the engineer was gone, his bed not slept in. Ten days later, Diesel's bloated body was found floating in the English Channel. The official cause of death was accidental drowning, but Diesel had suffered from mental breakdowns and economic setbacks, so suicide seemed a plausible alternative. Conspiracies, however, were shouted immediately across newspaper headlines. The British Secret Service murdered him to steal U-boat secrets, they said, or the Germans did him in to protect those secrets, or—most tantalizingly—the assassination was carried out by the titans of the oil trusts out of fear Diesel would put them out of business.

Here's to hoping that his engine—or something else—soon does.

BREEDS APART

Jack Russell was called the Sporting Parson because, while he may have been a reverend, his true calling was the hunt. Back in his final year at Oxford, Russell came across a milk-man with his doggie in tow, a white terrier with charming tan spots about her eyes and ears. Smitten, Russell bought little Trump on the spot. To his delight, Trump made a splendid hunting companion, gifted especially in rooting foxes out of their dens, and he used her to mother the breed that would take his name. The Jack Russell exempli-fies all things terrier—tenacity, feisty aggressiveness, and intelli-gence—and takes those traits to the extreme.

Louis Dobermann wanted an extreme sort of dog himself—extremely terrifying. Dobermann's motives were partly professional, the industrious German being a night watchman and tax collector, dangerous jobs both. However, it was in his third capacity, as town dogcatcher, that he had access to the breeds he needed to get the right mix of temperament, appearance, and that all-important size. It is unknown exactly which breeds Dobermann made use of, but somewhere in the genetic stew were the German pinscher, German shepherd, Great Dane, and rottweiler, which should give you some idea of the kind of animal he was aiming for. The result of Dobermann's efforts was Bismarck, the ultimate Hund from Hell, a black bitch whose offspring were a major hit with the German people.

dra·co·ni·an *adj. Cruel, harsh, severe.*

Draco was an Athenian lawmaker who drew up a seriously nasty penal code sometime around 621 B.C. The crotchety Draco was pro–death penalty to the extreme: Among qualifying offenses under his edicts were murder, treason, sacrilege, petty theft, and "idleness." When questioned if maybe death wasn't a bit too harsh for petty crimes, Draco reportedly said the *real* shame was that he couldn't prescribe anything worse for the bigger ones.

Draco's laws were posted for all to see on *axones*, wooden pyramids that spun around like magazine racks. For people to know what the laws even were was an innovation back then, let alone to have them written down. This benevolent reform notwithstanding, Draco and his laws were intensely hated.

dunce *n. A dullard; a dolt; a dum-dum. Duh.*

John Duns Scotus was a Scottish theologian and one the most influential thinkers of the Middle Ages. An ardent follower of Saint Francis, Duns Scotus spent his career at the universities of Oxford, Paris, and Cologne. He provided the definitive argument on the then culture-war issue of the Immaculate Conception, after which it became Catholic dogma that Mary was conceived without sin. For his delicately shaded approach to this and similar difficult issues he earned the nickname Doctor Subtilis, and his

John
DUNS
Scotus

theories held sway from his 1308 death through the end of the Middle Ages.

Duns Scotus's followers, the Scotists, dominated theology until another gang of scholars, the Thomists (after Thomas Aquinas), encroached on their turf. These new philosophers ridiculed the hairsplitting sophistry of Dr. Subtilis and his Dunsmen, who were impervious to learning anything new and different. The Scotists reacted reactionarily, resisting any change that threatened their preeminence. But their creed lost cred, and in the intellectual rumble of the Renaissance the elegant theories of Duns Scotus were knifed on account of his blockhead followers, and so to be called a dunce became the worst insult a would-be man of letters could receive, the irony of which would have been painfully obvious to Dr. Subtilis, if not the Dunsmen themselves.*

frick and frack *n. 1. A closely linked or inseparable pair. 2. A couple of morons.*
The Ice Follies was the original skating extravaganza, having among its galaxy of stars such luminaries as the British beauty Belita, Richard "Mr. Debonair" Dwyer, and the Swiss skating duo Werner Groebli and Hans-Rudi Mauch, better

---

* *Duns*, by the way, is pronounced the same as *dunce*, its spelling an obsolete convention also seen in *ones* and *twys* (*once, twice*).

known as Frick and Frack. Something like Siegfried and Roy with a sense of humor, in their signature move the "Clown Kings of the Ice" would skate at each other full steam and then, just as they were about to collide, short, stocky Frack would slide through the legs of tall, lanky Frick.

It brought down the house every time.

Frick and Frack got their shot at Hollywood stardom in 1943's *Silver Skates*, a movie about a traveling ice show facing bankruptcy, and the following year's *Lady, Let's Dance*, an ice-skating musical. (Note that a lot of actors—and screenwriters—were off fighting a war at the time.)

Frack was forced to retire in the mid-fifties due to health problems, but Groebli skated on for decades as Mr. Frick, delighting generations with his patented "cantilever spread eagle" trick.

fris·bee *n. A spinning circular disk used as a recreational device.*

In the 1930s, a couple of drunk Yale students munched down a pie and started playing catch with the leftover tin plate. The game took off, and soon the whole campus was eating pies and playing the new sport. Their pastry of choice was made by Mrs. Frisbie's Pies of Bridgeport, although it's unknown whether this preference speaks to the quality of her pastry or the aerodynamics of her tins, which came embossed with the company name. To signal the receiver that a flying object was coming at his head (which, being drunk, he might not notice), the thrower would yell "Frisbie!" the way a soldier shouts "Incoming!"

Mrs. Mary Frisbie was likely amused by this tossing around of her plates; certainly, her bakeries were selling a lot of pies—eighty thousand a day in 1956. On the other side of the country there was a guy who would've envied her: Fred Morrison had created a disk designed *specifically* for flying, but no one was buying them. Trying to cash in on the UFO craze, Morrison released the Pipco Flyin-Saucer, then the Pluto Platter, which caught the eyes of the Wham-O corporation. Wham-O had recently created the biggest fad America had ever seen, the Hula Hoop, selling twenty-five million units in four months. They purchased Morrison's designs, realizing why success had eluded him: His names all stunk. They soon learned there was already a better name for a flying disk—Frisbie—in a place where the sport was wildly popular. Wham-O decided to call their plastic version the same thing, but to trademark the name they changed the spelling to Frisb*ee*. (Very tricky.)

The Frisbee wound up being Wham-O's most popular and enduring product, but the word *frisbee*—however it's spelled—rightfully belongs to us all, or at the very least to those of us who have ever played it wasted on the quad.

Luigi
GALVANI

gal·va·nize *v. To shock or arouse into action.*

Luigi Galvani was a physician living in Bologna whose two seemingly diverse interests, physiology and electricity, combined into one after a spectacular accident.

One fine day in 1781, an assistant of the doc's touched a metal scalpel lightly to a nerve in the hip of a frog Galvani had dissected and, to his amazement, the dead amphibian's leg violently sprang to life. The other assistant swore it happened at the same moment he was cranking up sparks in the doc's nearby electricity machine. They called their boss over, and, with Galvani wielding the scalpel, managed to repeat the effect. The "wonderful phenomenon" caused a brainstorm in Galvani. (The same assistant later stuck his chocolate bar into the doc's peanut butter by mistake, but Galvani failed to see the possibilities of that *delizioso* combination.)

In a paper he presented in 1791, Galvani theorized that he had discovered a previously unknown electrical fluid produced in the brain that activated nerves and muscle. He called this force "animal electricity," but the process came to be known as galvanism, a term coined by Galvani's friend and intellectual rival, Alessandro Volta, who nevertheless disagreed with a key point of Galvani's conclusions.

For the rest of the story, see *voltage*.

ger·ry·man·der *v. To rezone voting districts to gain electoral advantage.*

Elbridge Gerry, a signer of the Declaration of Independence, offered his political credo at the Constitutional Convention of 1787. "The evils we experience flow from an excess of democracy. The people do not want virtue, but are dupes of pretended patriots." As if to test the theory, in 1812 Governor Gerry signed into law a Massachusetts redistricting bill aimed at helping his Republican party pick up state senate seats, an intention made clear in the grotesque appearance of one particularly convoluted voting district.

The story usually goes that Gilbert Stuart (the artist who painted pretty much every portrait of George Washington you've ever seen) entered the offices of the *Columbian Centinel*, where a map of the infamous district was hanging. Stuart went up to it and scribbled a head, wings, and claws onto the oddly shaped district. "That will do for a salamander!" the artist said. "Gerrymander!" said the editor. The problem with this tale is that the drawing that made the rounds in Federalist newspapers was later discovered to have been drawn—with great care—by the lesser-known illustrator Elkanah Tisdale.

Whatever the truth, the editorial cartoon had its desired effect, and to prove that people aren't total dupes (or at least back then weren't), the citizens of Massachusetts voted Gerry out of office.

SUPERVILLAINOUS

From kryptonite to Clark Kent, the Superman comics have bequeathed much to our culture. Little known, however, are the lexical contributions made by a pair of the Man of Steel's arch-enemies.

In the July 1958 issue of *Action Comics* (#242), writer Otto Binder introduced the evil intergalactic mastermind Brainiac. The villain shrank Metropolis and put it into a bottle, as he had done with other cities throughout the universe; Superman foiled his plan. With his lime-green skin, pink-and-white uniform, and short shorts, Brainiac was one of your less intimidating-looking supervillains. The word *brainiac*, an amalgam of *brain* and *maniac*, has entered the English language because, frankly, how could it not?

A few months after Brainiac debuted, another nemesis entered the picture in *Superboy* #58 (also written by the prolific Binder). Bizarro was the exact opposite of the last son of Krypton: His alter ego was Kent Clark, he belonged to the Injustice League, and his superpowers included freeze vision and X-ray hearing. He lived in Bizarro World, a square planet where life is the reverse of how it is on Earth. The word *bizarro* has come to mean an upside-down version of something or a creepy alternate reality, and was in part popularized by Superman überfan Jerry Seinfeld's eponymously titled "The Bizarro Jerry" episode of his eponymously titled sitcom *Seinfeld*.

graham crack·er *n. A type of cracker that is like a biscuit on its way to becoming a cookie.*

Before South Beach, before Dr. Atkins, there was Graham.

The Graham diet is vegetarian but not vegan; it allows for moderate intakes of dairy products and eggs, but the menu leans heavily on fruits, vegetables, and fiber. The centerpiece of this diet is graham flour, a whole-grain product that is dark, unsifted, and coarsely ground. Although it sounds as if it could be the latest diet craze in America, the Graham diet was in fact the first. But unlike today's dietary gurus, Sylvester Graham didn't care if people lost weight; he just wanted to bring them closer to God.

A Presbyterian minister and self-styled "physiological reformer," Graham created a dietary regimen that followed the ideals of the 1830s temperance movement and fought against what he saw as the evils of the Industrial Revolution. Graham railed against the dietary downside of consumer capitalism, denouncing chemical additives that millers put in flour to make it look more appealing. He promoted his whole wheat flour as a healthy alternative to a blanched product stripped of all its goodness, using it to create a digestive biscuit—the Graham cracker. Graham hoped his creation would help people avoid "stimulating" foods such as meat and spices, which he claimed produced gross amounts of lust in the body, and that his diet would in general lead to less sexual activity, which he was against in all but the most extenuating of circumstances.

Traveling the country to promote his ideas, Graham met with as much opposition as he did support. When he spoke butchers and bakers protested—so much so that he needed bodyguards to accompany him. While known derisively as Dr. Sawdust for his fibrous flour, Graham was revered among temperance types. Oberlin College mandated the adoption of his diet among students and faculty, even firing a professor who refused to stop bringing his own pepper shaker into the dining hall.

grog·gy *adj. Foggy in the brain, unsteady in the body.*

TO CAPTAINS OF THE SQUADRON!
Whereas the Pernicious Custom of the Seamen drinking their Allowance of Rum in Drams, and often at once, is attended by many fatal Effects to their Morals as well as their Health, the daily allowance of half a pint a man is to be mixed with a quart of water, to be mixed in one Scuttled Butt kept for that purpose.
—order of Vice Admiral Edward Vernon, commander of the British navy in the West Indies, August 12, 1740

At the time of the above edict, Edward "Old Grog" Vernon had just come off a career-making victory in the War of Jenkins' Ear, during which he captured the Spanish possession of Portobello. Although this made him a hero back home, he was hardly Mr. Popular with the sailors under his command once he ordered their rum rations cut. Thankfully, the effect of the grog, as the tars called the diluted spirit in dishonor of their commander, was still sufficient to render the men into the state described in the above definition.

guil·lo·tine *n. A beheading apparatus.*
In 1784 at Louis XVI's invitation the physician Joseph-Ignace Guillotin joined the commission to investigate Franz Mesmer; five years and a revolution later, Dr. Guillotin was elected to a rather different body, the Revolutionary *Assemblée nationale constituante*, where he proposed a method of execution that he believed to be both more dignified and, with its speedy efficiency, more humane. His suggestion was adopted, with vigor.

gup·py *n 1. A species of fish native to the Caribbean, often found swimming through plastic castles.*
This enduringly popular aquarium fish was named after the amateur Trinidadian zoologist R. J. Lechmere Guppy, quite possibly the most famous amateur Trinidadian zoologist of all time.

Dr. Joseph-Ignace

GUILLOTIN

guy *n. Am. slang: a way of referring to a male without having to call him a man.*

In the wee morning hours of November 5, 1605, Guy Fawkes was arrested in a rented storeroom under the House of Lords that was suspiciously packed with thirty-six barrels of gunpowder. Under torture, Guy confessed to being part of a Roman Catholic conspiracy to assassinate King James I, his family, and both houses of Parliament; he was hanged.

For over four hundred years, Guy Fawkes Day has been celebrated across the UK with fireworks and bonfires. On these crisp, late-autumn nights, children parade effigies of Fawkes through the streets chanting the nursery rhyme

> *Remember, remember the fifth of November,*
> *the gunpowder treason and plot.*
> *We see no reason why gunpowder treason*
> *should ever be forgot!*
>
> *Guy Fawkes, Guy Fawkes, t'was his intent*
> *to blow up King and parliament.*
>
> *Three score barrels were laid below*
> *to prove old England's overthrow.*
>
> *By God's mercy he was catch'd*
> *with a darkened lantern and burning match.*

So, holler boys, holler boys, let the bells ring.
Holler boys, holler boys, God save the King.

And what shall we do with him?
Burn him!

Upon reaching the great central bonfire, the kids toss "the guy" into the flames and then, if they are being traditional, follow it with an effigy of the pope.

Etymologically speaking, a *guy* came to mean someone of grotesque appearance, which came to include everyone, at least in America.

FIRST-NAME BASIS

Most first-name eponyms come from biblical characters, saints, or classical figures who are in general known only by a single name. In most other cases, words deriving from forenames are not eponyms but generic uses of common names—the more common the better—that tend to embody the everyman, or men, in the case of Tom, Dick, and Harry. True first-name eponyms are harder to come by, and even ones such as the above *guy* generally connote an average citizen, or one engaged in a profession, like the British bobby.

There are exceptions. A poindexter is a nerd, after the decidedly dorky cartoon character Poindexter (IQ: 222) of the *Felix the Cat* TV series. Yente Telebende was a loud-mouthed busybody in Jacob Adler's humorous essays about New York City's Lower East Side; the Yiddish first name became a Yiddish eponym, which shortly entered English as *yenta*, meaning a gossip or meddler.

Pet names are often given to the tools of war, be they ships, swords, or guns. The word *gun* itself, in fact, comes from Gunhild, a female Scandinavian name. If that sounds odd, consider that the Germans called their World War I Belgium-bashing supercannon *die dicke Bertha*—Fat Bertha—after Frau Bertha Krupp, owner of the armaments firm where they were manufactured. Our boys called them Big Berthas, and the Germans they were fighting, Jerry.

Bestowing a nickname upon the enemy is a common practice during wartime, from the Confederate Johnny Reb to the Viet Cong Charlie. An uglier but related practice are slurs such as mick for an Irishman, guido for an Italian, and nancy boy for an effeminate male.

Then there's sex. Men tend to be on a first-name basis with their penises, hence the terms dick, willie, and peter; condoms are jimmy hats or, in Britain, johnnies, where instead of horny you get randy and hanker for a right rogering. The sex of animals can also be told in a name. You have tomcats, a jackass and a jenny, and goats are divided into billies and nannies, the latter being a nickname for Anne or Agnes and also used to refer to long-term babysitters.

America's favorite name to represent the man on the street is Joe, be it Joe Blow, Joe Schmo, Joe Six-Pack, average Joe, or Joe the Plumber. Joe shows up in a number of other places, such as with sloppy joes and as a synonym for coffee, but the first name most pressed into lexical service—by a factor of absurdity—is my own.

As a noun used with the article *a, john* means the client of a prostitute; put *the* in front of it and you're talking about a toilet. In the past it had other meanings, among them a male servant, a policeman (shortened from "johndarm," as in *gendarme*), and a kind of plant. There is John Bull (the personification of England), John Barleycorn (the personification of liquor), John Q. Public, John Doe, the Dear John letter, and John Dory, a fish who for hundreds of years happily swam the seas as a dory before mysteriously acquiring a Christian name. You have Johnny-come-lately, Johnny-on-the-spot, and Johnny Crapaud (a Frenchman). Then there's Jack. A jack once meant a rough character, which is why those guys on the playing cards look so dodgy, but a jack was also a laborer, as in lumberjack, jack o'lantern (a night watchman), and jack-of-all-trades. By extension, a machine that replaced a worker was called a jack, like the device we use to raise things, which became a verb used in expressions such as to jack up and to jack off. In nineteenth-century America, the name came to be used as a form of address to strangers, as in, "Who you lookin' at, jack?" "You don't know jack shit" is an Americanism of later vintage. The Scottish variant Jock might be behind *jockstrap* and is certainly the reason a racehorse rider is called a jockey. The John phenomenon affects English via foreign words as well. In Venice the nickname Zanni is equivalent to Johnny; in the commedia dell'arte it was a generic name for any of the comedic male roles, those guys who acted zany.

We could go on, to jerry-rig, to jimmy a lock, to Jim Dandy, but let's ask ourselves instead—Jim, Jerry, Joe, John, Jack—how come all these names start with a J?

hook·er *n. Slang term for a prostitute; considered either vulgar or polite, depending on the company you keep.*

Fighting Joe Hooker was a hard-living leader beloved by his men. A veteran of the Seminole wars and the invasion of Mexico, he had trouble adjusting to civilian life, where his drinking and gambling wasn't quite so well tolerated as around the battle camp, and so was happy when the Civil War came along and offered him a chance to get back into the fighting game.

At the disaster of Antietam, Hooker distinguished himself by fighting the great Confederate general Stonewall Jackson to a standstill. Then came the further disaster of Fredericksburg, during which Union commander General Ambrose Burnside (see *sideburns*) ordered more than a dozen assaults by Hooker's brigade over the protests of Fighting Joe, who correctly recognized their inferior position. His troops fell in droves, and the never-shy Hooker called Burnside a "wretch" and his battle plan "preposterous," helping to get the general fired and himself promoted.

Having suffered a succession of lamblike commanders, Fighting Joe was precisely the kind of man Lincoln was looking for. Upon Hooker's appointment to the overall command of the Army of the Potomac, Union soldiers rejoiced. "May God have mercy on General Lee," Hooker said, "for I will have none." His modest plan for the spring

campaign was to engage and defeat Lee's army and straight-away march on the Confederate capital of Richmond.

To map out his success in a pleasant atmosphere, Hooker surrounded himself with cronies and his army headquarters became something between a "bar-room and brothel." His soldiers, meanwhile, ran roughshod over every corner of Washington, D.C., in search of paid sex. It became such a problem for military police that Hooker ordered that prostitutes be restricted to an area of the city known as Murder Bay, where assumedly the local populace wasn't so prudish. This red-light district became known as Hooker's Division, and the word *hooker*, meaning prostitute (already a regional slang term), gained widespread currency.

As for how things went against General Lee: not well. The showdown between Hooker and the Gray Ghost at Chancellorsville became known as Lee's Perfect Battle, if that gives you some idea of the outcome. After the defeat Hooker, like Burnside, offered his resignation to Lincoln with the expectation that it wouldn't be accepted, and he, like Burnside, received an unpleasant surprise from Honest Abe.

hoo·li·gan *n. A ruffian.*

A fixture around Southwark, a nineteenth-century Irish slum in London, Patrick Hooligan worked as a bouncer at neighborhood pubs. He was better known, however, as the mentor of young hoodlums, whom he instructed in the arts of robbery and assault. One day, old Paddy got into an argument with a bobby, killed him, and dumped the body in a garbage cart. Hooligan was nabbed and died soon after in prison, but his life's work was carried on by numerous London street gangs who bore his name and by soccer fans in stadiums across the land.

ja·cuz·zi *n. A whirlpool bath. v. To take one.*

In the beginning, Candido Jacuzzi just wanted to help his son. The poor boy suffered from severe rheumatoid arthritis and his only relief came from the hydrotherapy treatments he received at the hospital. In order to give his child round-the-clock whirlpool access, Jacuzzi developed a portable pump that could be placed into a bathtub. Being an engineer, he had the skills to do this; as co-owner of a Northern California manufacturing company, he had the capability. He and his six older brothers had started making aircraft equipment in 1915, but with the J-300 the Jacuzzis entered a new field.

Roy Jacuzzi had more vision than his uncle Candido and better marketing acumen. He smelled opportunity for the J-300 in late 1960s California and repackaged it as a stand-alone product he dubbed the Roman Bath. Sales were so good that a larger model, the Adonis, was introduced in 1970, followed by Jacuzzi's great breakthrough, the multi-person Gemini unit, available in a wide array of colors and swanky styles.

Swinging changed forever.

jan·i·tor *n. A man who pushes a cart of cleaning supplies down the halls of an institutional building.*
Pity poor Janus, once the mightiest Roman deity of all. He was the father of the gods—until his worshippers fell all over themselves for the flashier, sexier Greek pantheon and left Janus to be god of doors. (Those who attended to him—that is, doorkeepers—were called janitors.) Janus was well suited to his task, at least, having a face on both the front and back of his head. Romans believed this also allowed the god to see into both the future and the past, and for this reason Janus presided over the month that opened and closed each year.

January was a late entry to the Roman calendar, added at the same time as February. For centuries there were only ten months, winter being deemed unworthy of month-hood since nothing grew then. With the exception of February, the first four of the original months were, like January, named after deities: March for Mars, April for Apru (an Etruscan

IANVARIVS

SOLIS	LVNAE	MARTIS	MERCVRII	IOVIS	VENERIS	SATVRNI
	I	II	III	IV	V	VI
	CALENDS				NONES	
VII	VIII	IX AGONALS	X	XI	XII	XIII
						IDES
XIV	XV	XVI	XVII	XVIII	XIX	XX
XXI	XXII	XXIII	XXIV	XXV	XXVI	XXVII
			PAGANALIA!			
XXVIII	XXIX	XXX	XXXI			

borrowing of Aphrodite), May for Maia (a Roman earth goddess), and June for Juno (Jupiter's wife). The rest of the months were simply numbered, which—once the first of January was set as the official start to the year—created the odd situation of the ninth through twelfth months being named for the Latin numbers seven through ten, that is, *Septem*ber, *Octo*ber, *Novem*ber, *Decem*ber. And we would still have the summer months of *Quint*ilis and *Sext*ilis if not for a couple of emperors named Julius Caesar and Caesar Augustus.

The Romans didn't end with months when it came to honoring their deities. They believed that the planets represented gods who kept a rotating watch over the mortal coil as they crossed the sky. When the Romans adopted the seven-day week, they named the days after whichever god had the first shift of the morning. Conveniently, there were exactly seven planets according to ancient astronomy: Sol (the sun), Luna (the moon), Mars, Mercury, Jove (another name for Jupiter), Venus (or Venere), and Saturn.

A person's temperament was believed to be shaped by whichever god ruled over his or her birth, making you either solar, lunar, martial, mercurial, jovial, venereal, or saturnine. The latter four adjectives remain consistent with their Latin meaning, with the exception of venereal, which, before it became inextricably linked with STDs, meant "inclined to be lascivious; addicted to venery or lust," which is pretty much how it got to be inextricably linked with STDs in the first place.

jum·bo *adj. Enormous; huge; really, really big.*

One fine morning in 1861, a little elephant awoke expecting to spend another day munching grass on the sunny savannah. Alas, he never would again. Captured by exotic animal traders, the unwitting pachyderm was shipped off to the Jardin des Plantes in Paris, where he spent the unhappy remainder of his calfhood. Skinny, sickly, and only four feet tall, he was unceremoniously swapped to the London Zoo for a rhinoceros.

Named Jumbo by his new zookeeper—it kind of sounded African—the elephant began to grow. And how could he not? His daily menu included two hundred pounds of hay, two bushels of oats, ten to fifteen loaves of bread, a barrel of potatoes (Jumbo did not bant), a bunch of onions, and many, many barrels of water, with an additional one of whiskey or ale on occasion, for his health. Who says you eat better in Paris than in London?

Jumbo, now enormous, became a hit with the crowds. He'd snatch up coins and peanuts in his trunk and give rides to the kiddies for pocket change, including a couple of young tykes named Winnie Churchill and Teddy Roosevelt. And then a man took a ride on his back who knew he could charge a whole lot more than a few measly shillings for the Jumbo experience.

In 1881, Phineas T. Barnum expanded his circus from two to an unprecedented three rings. Needing a star, P. T.

went out and bought seven tons of one. The outrage across Britannia was immediate and intense. Schoolchildren wrote letters of protest to Queen Victoria, who herself was outraged but couldn't do anything to reverse the ten-thousand-dollar sale. The London *Daily Telegraph* bemoaned how poor Jumbo would have no more shady walks in the park and instead be forced to "amuse the Yankee mob." The controversy resulted in a publicity bonanza for Barnum, who billed Jumbo as the largest elephant in the world. America was seized by Jumbomania. Every product imaginable was called Jumbo. There were Jumbo cigars, Jumbo trading cards, Jumbo fans—if something was big, it was Jumbo-sized! The new attraction sold more than a million dollars in tickets for Barnum's Greatest Show on Earth in the first year alone.

For Jumbo, stardom wasn't that great. In a self-destructive burst reminiscent of so many later celebrities, Jumbo ran wild one day in Canada and was killed by a train. Some say he was drunk, others that he was in a blind rage, while Barnum, ever the master of spin, claimed Jumbo had been struck down while bravely rescuing a baby elephant, pushing the little fellow out of the way of the locomotive at the last instant.

Jules
LÉOTARD

le·o·tard *n. A snugly fitting, stretchable one-piece garment worn by dancers, gymnasts, and 1980s exercise queens.*

When Jumbo arrived in Paris, there was another kind of circus phenomenon underway. Jules Léotard, the son of a gymnasium owner, was a novice acrobat when he hit upon a brilliant idea: how about, instead of doing his routine on fixed bars, he did it on bars that swung? On November 12, 1859, at the tender age of twenty-one, Léotard made his public debut at the Cirque-Napoleon in Paris, and in a single performance created an art form. As if by magic he passed from one bar to the other, and even executed midair somersaults between them. With his lady-killing looks and birdlike abilities, Léotard became an international super-star, inspiring a Jumbo-like assortment of merchandise as well as the 1867 song "The Daring Young Man on the Flying Trapeze." For his shows, Léotard redesigned the standard acrobat's maillot into a flesh-hugging one-piece that both allowed fluid motion and showed off his show-offable muscles. It became known as the leotard and quickly found use in other arenas, such as the ballet studios of Paris.

All this, and poor Jules died at thirty-one.

lynch *v. To execute, esp. by hanging, without due process.*

"If you were a settler there, and had no other law to defend you, you would be glad of the protection of Judge Lynch," Sir Charles Lyell reported in his 1849 book *A Second Visit to the United States of North America*. The Judge Lynch in question was a mythical figure on the frontier, the authority invoked in the meting out of justice where there was no authority, at least none that those doing the meting desired to consult.

The "Lynch law" brand of vigilantism justice was seen by many nineteenth-century folk as a positively good thing. In the early 1800s an old Virginia farmer named William Lynch took credit for having assembled the original Lynch men back in Revolutionary days; a 1780 compact later turned up explaining why. Citing bands of lawless malefactors who committed horse stealing, counterfeiting, and "other species of villainy," Lynch and his fellow subscribers to the pact promised that "if they will not desist from their evil practices we will inflict such corporeal punishment on him or them, as to us shall seem adequate." No bothersome interference from courts or judges needed.

Old Lynch was just the kind of redneck you'd expect to be behind the Lynch law. But there was another Lynch, a Quaker by the name of Charles, who might have been the original judge. The Quaker Lynch was a justice of the peace and militia leader in Revolutionary War Virginia who was involved in rounding up and arresting a ring of British sympathizers supposedly planning a loyalist uprising. The Tory prisoners were given summary trials and dealt sentences that included hanging and were retroactively approved by the state legislature a couple of years later, perhaps sowing the perception that Lynch laws had inherent legitimacy.

So which Lynch was it? Recent research points to Charles, who is on record for using both the terms "Lynch's law" (1782) and "lynching" in reference to himself. As for William, he wouldn't be the first guy to stretch the truth; today it might have netted him a book deal and a guest shot on Oprah. And as for the 1780 pact he and his men made, this agreement—quoted and reprinted far and wide over the years—was likely a hoax perpetrated by Edgar Allan Poe, in whose *Southern Literary Messenger* it first appeared.

mal·a·prop·ism *n. An absurd masseuse of language.*
Mrs. Malaprop was a character in *The Rivals*, a comedy that debuted on the London stage in 1775 and was a long-lived hit across the English-speaking world. The actresses who played Mrs. Malaprop would elicit peals of laughter from the audience with lines such as "He is the very pine-apple of politeness!" or "I am sorry to say, Sir Anthony, that my affluence over my niece is very small." (People would kind of laugh at anything back then.) The author, Richard Sheridan, modeled the character's surname on the French word *malapropos.*

THE MILLINER'S TRADE

The top hat ushered in the modern era of men's head wear with its introduction shortly before 1800. No man about town would go without one, but the problem was, they were so tall and unwieldy; what were you supposed to do with the hats once you took them off? With a few steel springs Frenchman Antoine Gibus rectified this problem, inventing the collapsible top hat, called an opera or crush hat, or a gibus.

William Coke II had a different solution: make the bloody thing shorter. Coke was sick and tired of all the goddamn tree branches knocking off his top hats when he took a horseback ride, so in 1850 he commissioned a more manageable and sturdier cap, which came to be known popularly as the bowler, after Thomas and William Bowler, the Southwark hatters who manufactured it. The name suited the hat and its bowllike shape, although the French, seeing a different silhouette, called it a *chapeau melon*.

In the U.S. the bowler was instead known as a derby, supposedly because Americans became aware of the style from English dandies attending the Epsom Derby. The derby was the premier event in horse racing, so much so that the name came to mean "race" in a variety of contexts, from Kentucky to roller. Its origin dates to a 1779 coin toss, when Edward Smith-Stanley, the twelfth Earl of Derby, flipped

Sir Charles Bunbury for the honor. (Rollerbunbury, anyone?) Although to this day a fashion must among women in the Andes, the bowler/derby eventually yielded to softer hats with manipulatable crowns and brims.

Fédora debuted in 1882 with Sarah Bernhardt in the title role, a part written expressly for her by Victorien Sardou. Sardou and Bernhardt would work together many times, most famously in *La Tosca* (later adapted by Puccini), but it was the hat-wearing Princess Fédora Romanoff who set off a craze, as many a female fan of Bernhardt took to the streets sporting a fedora in a statement of both fashion and women's liberation.

Similar to the fedora but with a narrower brim is the trilby, whose name also—bizarrely—derives from a play's titular female character. The hat was worn in the first London production of *Trilby*, adapted from the hugely bestselling 1894 George Du Maurier novel of the same name. Set in bohemian 1850s Paris, the story follows the beautiful young artist's model Trilby O'Ferrall as she falls under the control of the malicious, manipulative hypnotist Svengali. Normally, Trilby is tone-deaf, but under Svengali's mesmeric spell, she becomes singing sensation La Svengali. It ends badly.

Baseball cap aside, the most American of headwear is the cowboy hat, aka the stetson, although upon its introduction John B. Stetson called his product "The Boss of the Plains." Stetson recognized that a hat offering so much shade would provide welcome relief for the workingman out west. The stetson quickly became an indispensable part of the cowboy uniform and, in its ten-gallon variety, a symbol of Texas. If a man is "all hat and no cattle," he's wearing a stetson, even if only figuratively.

The need for shade on another frontier produced a different sort of hat. Improvised by British troops to keep the sun off their necks, the havelock is a cap with a hanging rear flap—think French Foreign Legion. The hat is named in homage to Major-General Sir Henry Havelock, who died of dysentery days after notching one of the most important British victories of the Indian Rebellion (a conflict previously known, when the winners named such things, as the Indian Mutiny).

Another military hat is the busby, by long-standing tradition said to be named after Dr. Richard Busby, a seventeenth-century headmaster so renowned for caning his charges that he appears in Alexander Pope's *Dunciad* "Dropping with Infant's blood." Entering the lexicon as a "large bushy wig" (referring to the sadistic headmaster's coif, perhaps?), the meaning of *busby* somehow switched reference to the tall and furry plumed hat of the much-copycatted Hungarian hussar.

Finally, there's the tam-o'-shanter, worn by every bagpipe player you've ever seen, with the tartan pattern and the toorie on top. The classic Scottish bonnet is named after a 1790 poem by Robert Burns, known in Scotland simply as the Bard. (William who?) The brilliant Burns wrote in a mixture of English and Scots dialect, the latter evident in the title of his "Auld Lang Syne." "Tam o' Shanter" recounts the late-night drunken ride of its title character. "Inspiring bold John Barleycorn! What dangers thou canst make us scorn!" it goes, and as Tam nears the kirk, he happens upon a witches' Sabbath. The party is in full swing, and Tam is particularly taken with the dancing of one scantily clad winsome witch: "[Tam] roars out, 'Weel done, Cutty-sark!' And in an instant, all was dark." The offended witches give chase, but just in time Tam's horse, Meg, makes the Brig o' Doon and the hellish legion vanishes, unable to cross the water.

(For those interested: *Tam* is a Scottish variant of Tom; *o' Shanter* identifies his town of origin; a *toorie* is a pom-pom; *auld lang syne* means "old long since," in the sense of "long ago"; a *kirk* is a church; "Weel done, Cutty-sark!" is akin to "Lookin' good, Hotpants!," *cutty* meaning short, as in cut off, and *sark* being Scots for shirt; and a *brig* is a bridge.)

mar·ti·net *n. A merciless disciplinarian; a stickler for rules regardless of circumstance.*

When Louis XIV ascended to the throne, French soldiery was a sorry lot. The ever-increasing importance of gunpowder-powered projectiles presented a particular challenge to the Gallic warrior, who exhibited a tendency to run the other way at the sound of it. The question was, How do you make men do something so stupid as hurl themselves headlong into a storm of cannon and musket balls? The answer: Bring on Jean Martinet, the original drill instructor.

King Louis made Martinet, who showed his mettle whipping the Régiment du Roi into shape, inspector general of the infantry in 1667, convinced that Martinet's extreme brand of drilling would turn his soldiers into the mindless lemmings he desired. With draconian severity, Martinet instilled discipline and efficiency while demanding absolute adherence to even the pettiest of rules, paving the way for the future Sergeant Hulkas of the world and turning the French infantry into a well-oiled machine—no mean feat. For this achievement Martinet gained fame across the continent and the enduring contempt of his men.

Martinet would not live long. The drillmaster was killed during the siege of Duisburg, when he was shot down by the "friendly fire" of his own perfectly trained, well-disciplined troops.

A last note. In French a *martinet* is a swallow, but also a kind of whip, similar to a cat-o'-nine-tails and excellent for scourging. Until recently, *martinets* were available in pet-supply stores in France but have since been removed as they were being used mostly on children. They do, however, remain top sellers in S&M shops. Speaking of which, see next.

mas·och·ism *n. The urge to derive pleasure from abuse and humiliation as administered by another or oneself, or one's sports team.*

Leopold von Sacher-Masoch was a writer in Hapsburg Austria of the generation that preceded Freud and Klimt. His signature work was *Venus im Pelz (Venus in Furs)*, about a man who becomes obsessed with a woman named Wanda; the more he loves her, the more he wants to be degraded by her, to the point that he begs to become her legal slave. They sign a contract in which he promises to do whatever Wanda asks, with the singular condition that she always wear furs. Sadly for the hero, Wanda falls in love with another man who isn't such a wuss.

Masoch's book is definitively kinky, although by today's standards (let alone those of his predecessor, de Sade) the sex scenes are demure, and the turgid prose is heavily weighted down by philosophical rambling. Masoch

Leopold
von
Sacher-MASOCH

exalts himself as a "supersensualist," identifying heavily with the Christian martyrs who gladly submitted to torture in return for elevated spirituality (see *tawdry*). The writer is at equal pains to explain his other fetish—a crazed obsession with furs—but does so rather less convincingly.

Venus im Pelz was based on a real-life affair, and after its publication Masoch became involved with a woman named Aurore Rümelin, who played out certain of his fantasies, including taking on the name of his character Wanda. Masoch entered into a contract with this Wanda which began with the salutation "My Slave" and ended with, "Should you ever find my domination unendurable and should your chains ever become too heavy, you will be obliged to kill yourself, for I will never set you free." The slave signed the document "Dr. Leopold, Knight of Sacher-Masoch."

Masoch and Aurore/Wanda married, but somehow things didn't work out.

mau·so·le·um *n. A large tomb, or a building containing several of them, or a big empty place that feels likes one.*
Mausolos was a Persian satrap who had a seriously nice tomb. In life, Mausolos expanded his family's influence into Greece and came into conflict with Athens. Upon his death, in 353 B.C., the building of a great memorial in Helicarnassus

was commissioned by Artemisia, who was doubly broken-hearted, being both Mausolos' widow and sister. (Those satraps liked keeping it all in the family.)

The Mausoleum of Mausolos would go on to be named one of the Seven Wonders of the Ancient World, the highest architectural prize pretty much ever. And for good reason. Not only was the tomb absurdly enormous, it was covered with statues and elaborate friezes carved by the finest Greek sculptors of the day.

The building stood for roughly sixteen centuries before being shattered by earthquakes. Soon after, the Knights of Malta scavenged the marble to fortify their nearby castle, took the sculptures they liked to decorate it, and ground and burned the rest into lime. Sadly, all that's left of the tomb is a bit of rubble, which if you're interested is somewhere in Turkey. The best of its remaining statuary, like so much of the world's great art, was carted off during the Victorian era and now sits in London's British Museum.

mav·er·ick *n. An individual who tends to his own individuality.*

Samuel Augustus Maverick was a Yale graduate, lawyer, Mexican War veteran, and San Antonio mayor who owned so much Texas real estate they named a county after him. In the mid-1840s, Maverick accepted a herd of cattle in

Sam MAVERICK

exchange for a debt and, not caring much for livestock, neglected them to the point of allowing calves to wander about unbranded, a cardinal sin in the free-ranging days before barbed wire. The lack of a brand became a brand in itself: Whenever anybody found a stray calf with no markings, they said, "That there's a maverick." Metaphorical uses soon followed.

A more famous owner of the surname was the fictional Old West hustler Bret Maverick, played by James Garner in an excellent 1950s TV show and by Mel Gibson in a less excellent 1990s movie.

men·tor *n. One who imparts experiential wisdom to those who have less of it.*

When Odysseus departed Ithaca to go fight the Trojan War, he left his young son, Telemachus, in the care of his wise friend Mentor. For the duration of the conflict and Odysseus' long sea-tossed voyage home, the aged Mentor advised the young prince and helped him fend off his mother Penelope's legion of suitors.

The mythology surrounding the Trojan War era has resulted in an all-time bounty of eponyms. While terms like *Achilles' heel* and *odyssey* might still be used with an idea of the events to which they refer, certain words have become so deeply ingrained as to have broken free of their original context entirely, such as with *siren*, the use of which as a device for making noise dates only to the nineteenth century, and *hector*, which evolved from meaning a valiant warrior in the mold of the great Trojan prince to a bully and a braggart, from which it became a verb meaning "to domineer."*

Many such eponyms, however, are fading altogether—along with our collective educations. One is *myrmidon*, the name of the race of men descended from ants (yeah, *ants*) who were Achilles' staunchest supporters, thus any member of an entourage or gang. *Stentorian* derives from the "great-lunged" Stentor, whose voice Homer describes as crying out "with the blast of fifty other men," while a cassandra, ignored predictor of bad fortune, was coined after the doomsayer none of the Trojans believed.

mes·mer·ize *v. To spellbind or enthrall; to captivate.*
Franz Anton Mesmer studied medicine in Vienna, writing his 1766 doctoral dissertation on the gravitational effects of the planets on the body, a theory then in vogue. Mesmer went on to become a successful physician with a unique way of curing people: He would have them swallow a solution of iron, then pass magnets over their bodies to summon an "artificial tide" that helped unblock the free flow of "life fluid." Blocked life fluid, you see, is bad.

---

* My own wife is named after Hector's bride, the princess of Troy, Andromache. Hi, honey.

Franz Anton
MESMER

Dr. Mesmer soon discovered that he needn't resort to outside devices as he had his own "animal magnetism"* to get life fluids flowing. After an unfortunate incident with a blind girl, he moved to Paris, where the practice of Mesmerism became a sensation. With a process of laying on hands, hypnosis, and suggestion set to the otherworldly sounds of a glass harmonica (later used in a thousand horror movies), Mesmer produced trance states in his patients that provoked convulsions, the desired "crisis" that uncorked blockages. His mass healings became a happening.

Louis XVI appointed a crack medical commission to investigate Dr. Mesmer, gathering such luminaries as U.S. ambassador Benjamin Franklin, creator of Mesmer's beloved glass harmonica, and—somewhat ironically for the monarch—a certain Dr. Guillotin. Their verdict: *merde*.

nic·o·tine *n. Addictive substance found in tobacco; also used as an insecticide.*

In 1560, ambassador to Portugal Jean Nicot sent a little something from the New World to the French court back home as a gift: tobacco. Much as they later would with Dr. Guillotin's suggestion, the French took to the new idea enthusiastically.

---

* This phrase, coined by Mesmer, had nothing to do with animals but with *anima*, the Latin word for soul.

Jean NICOT

onan·ism *n. Masturbation.*

Genesis 38 opens with Israelite tribal leader Judah espying a pretty young Canaanite; Judah "took her, and went in unto her," after which event she conceived Er, and, after another going-in-unto, Onan.* When the time came Judah married off his eldest son, but Er "was wicked in the sight of the LORD; and the LORD slew him." So Judah said to Onan, his second son, "Go in unto thy brother's wife, and marry her, and raise up seed to thy brother"—meaning, give your dead brother an heir. Onan, while fully on board with the sex part, didn't cotton to the idea of being stepfather to his own child, so after he went in unto his brother's wife, he pulled out, and spilled his seed all over the ground. "And the thing which he did displeased the LORD: wherefore he slew him also."

That's all we know about Onan. So how is it that the name of this randy and unscrupulous Israelite came to be synonymous with masturbation? That's where things get weird.

That Onan was killed because he had sex with his sister-in-law under false pretenses seems the obvious reading of Genesis 38, but from early days an alternate interpretation took hold that the Lord was smiting Onan for the wasteful act of spilling seed itself, and therefore any spilling of seed (you get that by "seed" we're talking semen here, right?) without impregnating intentions was verboten.

---

* Rhymes with Conan, as in O'Brien, not the Barbarian.

Then came *Onania, or the Heinous Sin of Self-Pollution, and All Its Frightful Consequences in Both Sexes, Considered*, an early-eighteenth-century bestseller that claimed "onanism" was the cause of gonorrhea, blindness, insanity, and stunted growth. It offered as cures "Strengthening Tincture" and "Prolifick Powder," expensive at ten and twelve shillings apiece, but how can you put a price on being master of your domain? Though transparent quackery, *Onania* piqued the interest of Dr. Samuel Auguste Tissot, a well-respected Swiss medical researcher. After intently studying many young male masturbators, Tissot concluded in his 1760 work *L'Onanisme* that semen was an "essential oil" that, when expelled from the body in unnecessary amounts, caused a plethora of disastrous medical conditions, legitimizing *Onania* and causing boys everywhere to fear that masturbation led not only to eternal damnation but to disfigurement and death.

Thanks a lot, doc.

WORDS OF BIBLICAL PROPORTIONS

The Bible is our single most fecund source of eponyms. Whether or not these words are anonyponymous depends upon one's familiarity with the good book, so, with the exception of Onan, these eponyms have been excluded from our main list of entries. But for those of you who never went to Sunday school, here's a sampling.

Jezebel was the Yoko Ono of the Old Testament, a Phoenician princess who married Ahab, king of Israel, and got him to ditch Yahweh in favor of her hometown god, Baal. For this, *jezebel* has forever after stood for any manner of conniving, shameless, brazen, controlling, impudent hussy.

The Old Testament produced a surfeit of synonyms for *giant*, from *goliath* to *behemoth*, the largest creature on land (thankfully an herbivore) and *leviathan*, the greatest beast of the sea (eating preferences unspecified). A *jeremiad* is a litany of woes and/or complaints, a reference to the prophet Jeremiah's aptly titled Book of Lamentations. Nimrod was a "mighty hunter before the Lord" in Genesis, yielding the expected meaning of one skilled in the catch, but another use, as a contemptible moron, comes from Bugs Bunny's sarcastic belittling of Elmer Fudd. Bugs also popularized another O.T. eponym, *methuselah*, meaning a really old guy, after the great-great-great-grampa of Nimrod, who lived to the ripe old age of 969.

The New Testament gave us a doubting Thomas and a good Samaritan, plus a not-so-good Samaritan, Simon Magus, the first heretic; *simony* is the buying and selling of church offices. A *judas* needs no explaining, but how Mary Magdalene came to be an eponym does.

In Middle English Mary Magdalene was called Maudelen, and she was most often depicted weeping piteously over the dead Christ. Then, as now, there were lots of sentimental old drunks across England, and when they began to cry into their beer they were said to be acting all Maudelen, which is to say, *maudlin*.

pan·der *v. To cynically cater to another's interests.*

The character from whom this term originates has a long and varied history on the margins of great literature. In Homer's *Iliad*, Pandarus was a Trojan archer who played a pivotal role in the conflict, breaking a truce with the Greeks by firing off a hasty arrow. The medieval romance of Troilus and Cressida, however, found Pandarus performing a rather different function.

First, about Troilus. He was the little brother of the Trojan princes Hector and Paris, known mostly for having been really good-looking and getting whacked by Achilles. Homer mentions his name only in passing. In the Middle Ages, however, this bit player suddenly became the protagonist of a great love story. No longer just some pretty boy, Troilus valiantly battles Achilles, wounding him, and even routs his fearsome Myrmidons. The crux of the drama is Troilus's love for Cressida, who is being held prisoner by Troilus's father, Priam, in retaliation for her father's desertion. Troilus needs someone to help him get to Cressida. Enter Pandarus.

Pandarus is Troilus's friend and the uncle of the imprisoned Cressida; taking pity on the lovesick Trojan prince, Pandarus acts as Troilus's go-between in wooing the girl. At least, this is how the story went by the time the twelfth-century *Roman de Troie* got retold by Boccaccio (1330s) and re-retold by Geoffrey Chaucer, from whose *Troilus and*

Criseyde (1380s) the name popularly entered our language. A "pandare" meant a helper in secret love affairs, but the term soon took on a more negative, pimplike connotation, so much so that when Shakespeare wrote *his* version of *Troilus and Cressida* (c. 1602) he made Pandarus a cynical degenerate merrily willing to procure his niece for the Trojan prince. The Bard also endowed the character with a remarkable degree of self-conscious prescience:

> *Since I have taken such pains to bring you together, let all pitiful goers-between be called to the world's end after my name, call them all — Pandars!*

pants *n. Pants.*
Pantaleon was an unmarried physician living in the pagan Byzantine empire who, by simply invoking the name of Jesus Christ, could perform miraculous acts such as healing a blind man. Jealous, Pantaleon's fellow doctors denounced him to the emperor, who, himself a patient of Pantaleon's, asked the good doctor to give up this Christian nonsense — whereupon Pantaleon proved the power of God by curing a man of paralysis. Having witnessed the trick, the emperor condemned Pantaleon to death for the practice of black magic.

As is the case with many Catholic martyrs, death was the beginning of a second life. Pantaleon became the

patron saint of physicians, bachelors, and torture victims, and now his own name could be invoked to cure a variety of ailments, as well as to guard against locusts. A member of the Fourteen Holy Helpers—a sort of league of super-saints who banded together to fight the Black Death—Saint Pantaleon's stock went up dramatically in places like hard-hit Venice, where a spectacular church was dedicated to him in thanks for delivering the city from the plague. He later won even more ardent veneration in the Serenissima with the advent of the lottery and his designation as the heavenly provider of winning numbers. San Pantalone became so identified with the city in fact that his name was borrowed by the commedia dell'arte for the character of the prototypically greedy Venetian merchant.

The commedia dell'arte had storylines harking back to Roman times but was played out as improvisational farce. Each actor of the troupe dressed in mask and costume as one of a repertory of stock characters, such as Arlecchino, easily recognizable in his trademark diamond-patch outfit and better known to us by his Frenchified name, Harlequin. The costume signature of Pantalone was a pair of red leg-gings that reached the feet, a distinctively Venetian man-ner of cladding the legs that audiences outside the Veneto found odd and remarkable. Over the years and in various languages, the character's name was borrowed to describe varying fashions of long trousers and related garments. This makes it hard to pin down exactly how and when American English adapted the anglicized name Pantaloon, but by the mid-1800s the term had comfortably been shortened to *pants*. Around this same time women first began wearing bloomers, which were advocated as an advancement in women's freedom (quite literally, as it was seriously hard to move in those hoop skirts), most passionately by women's rights and temperance activist Amelia Jenks Bloomer.

pa·pa·raz·zi *n. A member of the media who stalks celebrities.*

On his trip to Calabria in the winter of 1897–1898, English novelist George Gissing stopped for a few nights in Catanzaro, staying at the Baedeker-recommended Albergo Centrale. In his room he found a printed card addressed to guests.

"The proprietor," Gissing later summarized the note, "had learnt with extreme regret that certain travellers who slept under his roof were in the habit of taking their meals at other places of entertainment. This practice, he desired it to be known, not only hurt his personal feelings—*tocca il suo morale*—but did harm to the reputation of his establishment. Assuring all and sundry that he would do his utmost to maintain a high standard of culinary excellence, the proprietor ended by begging his honourable clients that they would bestow their kind favours on the restaurant of the house . . . and therewith signed himself—Coriolano Paparazzo."

Sixty years later a screenwriter in Rome was beset by a different problem. Ennio Flaiano was working with director Federico Fellini on a movie about international society and the nightlife of the Via Veneto. Their protagonist was a reporter who had an ever-present companion, a character based on the brazen new breed of photographer who made a living shooting stealth photos of celebrities on the town. The problem was what to call him. Flaiano desperately wanted the perfect name, a name that would make the character come alive. By chance, he opened up a new Italian translation of Gissing's 1901 travel book *By the Ionian Sea* to a random page and saw the peculiar surname of the owner of the Albergo Centrale. "Paparazzo," Flaiano wrote in his notes, "the name of the photographer will be 'Paparazzo.' "

The movie, *La Dolce Vita*, was a smash success, and in its plural Italian form the word *paparazzi* has entered the world lexicon, giving old Coriolano a reputation he never expected. As Flaiano summed up, "Names have their destiny."

pas·qui·nade *n. The public ridiculing of a person in written verse or prose.*

Piazza Navona was one of Rome's most fashionable addresses long before the Via Veneto, and going way back was the site of the Stadium of Domitian, the field of which is traced in the piazza's unusual oval shape. The badly damaged statue of a warrior thought to have decorated the Circus Agonalis (as the stadium was also known) came unearthed in 1501 when a street was dug up for the rebuilding of the Palazzo Orsini. Although such fragments were a dime a dozen in the Eternal City, the elderly cardinal overseeing the work was so charmed by the marble torso that he had it erected on the corner of the palazzo where it had been found.

Almost immediately, signs began appearing around the neck of the statue, who acquired the nickname Pasquino after maybe a tailor or barber who lived in the neighborhood. These nocturnally affixed placards contained bitingly sarcastic verses attacking the most powerful men of Rome, most often the ruling pope, at least one of whom tried to have Pasquino hurled into the Tiber. Not that it would've mattered, as statues all across the city had begun "talking," a custom that continues to this day.

pi·la·tes *n. A very expensive form of exercise.*

Life was tough growing up in 1880s Germany with a name like Pilates. *Pontius Pilate, Killer of Christ!* was the sort of taunt little Joseph Pilates had to put up with from kids in the school yard, made worse by the fact he was the classic sickly child, burdened with a plethora of diseases, both medieval (rickets, rheumatic fever) and modern (asthma). But Joseph turned it all around like the ninety-pound weakling in a Charles Atlas ad by throwing himself into bodybuilding, yoga, gymnastics, and boxing, coming up with his own system to strengthen and develop key muscles. Pilates came to America in the 1920s and soon opened a studio in New York. His "Contrology" method first caught on in the dance community, attracting such luminaries as Martha Graham and George Balanchine. It would take more than half a century, however, for Pilates to hit the mainstream (assuming, of course, that you consider status-conscious bougie housewives the mainstream). Once it did, the method became so popular that competing schools went to court over whether Pilates was a brand or *pilates* was a word.

A generic term for a product cannot be trademarked; in fact, a trademark can be invalidated if a product is so successful that its name *becomes* generic. This was enshrined into law when Judge Learned Hand stripped the German company Bayer of its exclusive right to the word aspirin, which it had trademarked in 1899. Brands whose parent

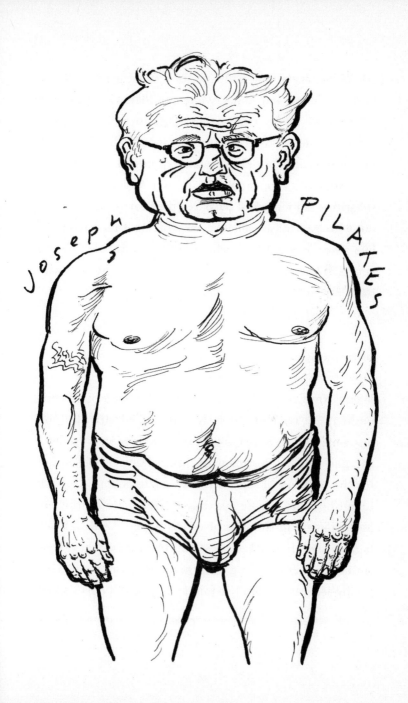

companies have long had to fight against genericide are Coke, Kleenex, and Xerox, while nowadays Google works to stop the media from using *google* to mean doing an Internet search. Otherwise their brands might go the way of *zipper*, called "hookless fasteners" until B. F. Goodrich came out with Zipper galoshes in 1923; *heroin*, a morphine substitute trademarked by Bayer the year before it came out with aspirin (so-called because taking it made you feel like a hero); and *pilates*, which in 2000 was ruled by the courts to be free for anyone to use. At least, those of us who can afford it.*

pom·pa·dour *n. A coiffure in which the hair is brushed high off the forehead and turned back in a roll.*

Jeanne Antoinette Poisson was a hot number around Paris in the 1740s, no matter that she was saddled with a kid and husband. Seeing her stock on the rise, Jeanne's "uncle," the powerful Le Normant de Tournehem, proposed her for the position of royal mistress, going behind the back of her husband, whose marriage to Jeanne de Tournehem had arranged in the first place. As hoped, Louis XV fell hard for her; in quick succession, the king bought Jeanne the estate of Pompadour, made her a marquise, and had her legally separated from her fuming husband. Louis also let

---

* For trademarks staving off genericide, see *frisbee, jacuzzi,* and *tupperware*; for one already expired, see *zeppelin*.

Jeanne Antoinette Poisson
de
POMPADOUR

her run the country's foreign policy: She favored a shift in allegiance from the tiresome Prussians to the more stylish Hapsburgs, a move that resulted in the Seven Years' War, a conflict which was, even by French standards, an utter disaster. (The days of Martinet were, sadly for the French, long gone.) Pompadour was blamed for the debacle and vilified but today is more fondly remembered as having bequeathed her name to a really silly fifties hairstyle.

pro·crus·te·an *adj. Ruthlessly forcing others to conform to one's own arbitrary standards.*

Procrustes ran a hostelry on the side of an empty country road that led to Athens. A conscientious host, he made sure every guest fit his bed exactly; if they were too short for it, Procrustes would have them stretched out on the rack; if they were too tall, he'd lop off part of their legs. The thing was, the bed was adjustable, the game rigged. The Attic hero Theseus turned the tables on Procrustes when he put the criminal to his own bed and, finding him too long, lopped off both his feet and head, permanently closing Procrustes's peculiar B&B.

pyg·ma·lion *n. A svengali without the malevolent intentions.*

A rather different mythological character from Procrustes was Pygmalion. According to Ovid, Pygmalion was a sculptor who carved for himself the ideal woman. His statue was so realistic that Pygmalion fell in love to the point of bringing her little gifts and putting a pillow under her head when he lay her down to bed. Pygmalion prayed to Venus for a wife like his ivory girl, and the goddess, understanding what the sculptor really wanted, transformed his creation into flesh and blessed the marriage.

Taking inspiration from Ovid's tale, George Bernard Shaw's *Pygmalion* features the phoneticist Henry Higgins, who makes a bet that he can transform the speech of Cockney flower girl Eliza Doolittle to the point where he can pass her off as a duchess. In the third act, Eliza utters the line, "Walk! Not bloody likely." At the time, *bloody* was not a quaint Britishism but something more akin to *fuck*, replaced with euphemisms like *blasted*, *blooming*, and *blinking*. When the word was used onstage, it caused a sensation. (Shaw even wrote in his stage direction, "[Sensation].") *Pygmalion* became a synonym for curse word, and people began to say "not pygmalion likely" and "pygmalion hell!" Though this use had faded from the language, pygmalion, in the sense of a person who attempts to mold the behavior of another, endures.

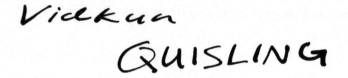

Vidkun QUISLING

quis·ling *n. The native puppet of an occupying power.*

Vidkun Quisling was the son of a pastor and Norway's premier fascist. He formed the Nasjonal Samling Party in 1933 with the aim of becoming Norway's first Fører. What he was selling, however, Norwegians weren't buying; few joined his lonely party, and a measly 2 percent was his best showing at the polls. Frustrated by his countrymen, Quisling met Hitler to ask him if he would please invade his homeland, a request his hero promptly granted. When fascist troops arrived on Norwegian soil in April 1940, Vidkun seized the day and announced a coup over the radio.

Hitler didn't return his devotee's ardor, considering Quisling a loser, and removed him from power at once; however, a Reichskommisar proved little more popular than a Quisling, and Vidkun was named premier of the puppet government in 1942, a post he lasted in until his arrest in 1945. He was the same year executed, a feat not easily accomplished in any Scandinavian country, particularly one lacking the death penalty.

The adoption of the word *quisling* spread fast into languages across the continent and beyond, putting Vidkun in the rarified company of Judas Iscariot and Benedict Arnold as men so vilified that their very name means traitor. Vidkun, however, is the only one obscure enough to have had his name decapitalized.

rit·zy *adj. High-class; fancy.*

César Ritz was just another country bumpkin who came to the big city to work as a waiter, but unlike the rest of us he put his heart into it. Already by age nineteen "César le rapide" had risen to be maître d'hôtel at the posh Chez Voisin in Paris, where his legend as tastemaker to the wealthy began. It grew exponentially as he managed hotels across belle epoque Europe, most fortuitously Monaco's Grand Hotel, where Ritz met chef Auguste Escoffier. Escoffier had worked his way up through the finest kitchens in France, including a brief stint as the chef de cuisine of the French army during the Franco-Prussian war. (It might've gone better had the troops been hungrier, as the conflict was, even by the lowest of French standards, an epic catastrophe.)

Ritz and Escoffier became a team, and their decade of success at London's Savoy Hotel emboldened César to lease a palace on the Place Vendôme, the most fashionable square in Paris, and open the Hotel Ritz in 1898. Its success was instantaneous and sensational, and *Ritz* itself became the international byword for luxury. "Putting on the Ritz" meant to dress up swell, and the verb *to ritz* meant to put on airs. It could also have meant to reach the pinnacle of your profession and then suffer a complete mental breakdown, which is what happened to poor César, who would spend the last two decades of his life in convalescence while Escoffier cemented his reputation as the greatest French chef in history.

ORIGINAL RECIPES

In 1892–1893, one of the guests at the London Savoy was the great soprano Nellie Melba; during this time Escoffier is credited with naming not one but *two* famous dishes after her. Melba toast hardly needed Escoffier's genius to be invented; when Nellie had a spell under the weather it was the one thing she could eat, but with Escoffier's imprimatur even this blandest of items took on the sheen of high elegance. Rather more rich is the dessert he created in the diva's honor, peach melba.

Examples of epicurean homages abound, from General Tso's chicken to beef carpaccio, named after a nineteenth-century military man from Hunan province and a Renaissance-era painter from Venice, respectively. Rarer is the case of the honoree actually having something to do with the dish named after him or her, but they do exist.

A year or so after Melba's stay at the Savoy, a young stockbroker on the opposite side the pond walked into another storied hotel, the Waldorf, nursing a wicked hangover. To make himself feel better, Lemuel Benedict, like Dame Nellie, ordered toast, except Benedict asked for it to be loaded with bacon and a poached egg, plus some hollandaise sauce on the side, please. Knowing a good thing when he saw one, the Waldorf's young maître d'hôtel, Oscar

Tschirky, substituted ham and an English muffin for bacon and toast and put eggs Benedict on the hotel menu. Oscar of the Waldorf (as he would become known) stayed on the job fifty years and, though not a chef, created veal Oscar and the Waldorf salad, made Thousand Island dressing an American staple, and wrote a bestselling cookbook.

Thirty years later, over on the West Coast, Prohibition would prove a boom time for Mexico, as Americans who wanted to liquor up legally had to travel south of the border to party. Cesare Cardini, an Italian restaurateur in San Diego, saw the opportunity and opened a restaurant in Tijuana, where in 1924 he created a salad of romaine lettuce, croutons, and Parmesan cheese with an olive-oil-and-egg-based dressing (but no anchovies). Caesar's salad became a favorite among the movie-star set, who brought it back home with them.

Another imported dish with a Hollywood imprimatur dates to the 1920 marriage of Douglas Fairbanks to Mary Pickford, the original Brangelina. For their honeymoon, the bride and groom visited Rome, where they stopped one night at the restaurant of Alfredo di Lelio. They fell in love with his signature fettuccine dish and, like many an American before and since, came home from Italy raving about the food they ate. But unlike for the rest of us, other people cared. (You can still get a fettuccine Alfredo at di Lelio's restaurant; the authentic version is made with heaps of butter and Parmesan cheese.)

The latter half of the roaring twenties saw two Brown Derby eateries open in Los Angeles. The original was a diner constructed in the shape of a hat, but the second, more upscale version became headquarters for the great stars of the day. One of its owners, Bob Cobb, raided the Derby's fridge late one night, chopping up what he could find into a salad. Whether the snack he made was for himself or for Clark Gable, as varying legends have it, the Cobb salad would become Hollywood's homegrown dish of fame.

sa·dism *n. The urge to derive pleasure from the abuse and humiliation of another; cruelty.*

Donatien Alphonse François, the Marquis de Sade, was born in 1740 to one of the oldest families of French nobility. At a young age he began a military career that would last until the end of the Seven Years' War, at which point he married a loving woman who would bear him three children.

In 1768, de Sade decided to celebrate Easter Sunday by bringing home a beggar woman to imprison, sexually assault, and torture. Though the incident landed him in jail, the marquis saw no reason to repent. In 1772, he had an orgy with a male servant, a couple of prostitutes, and a pillbox of Spanish fly. It was all going swimmingly until the girls became convinced that the aphrodisiac was making them sick, and de Sade found himself sentenced to death for sodomy and poisoning. Though he escaped execution, the rest of the marquis's life was a merry-go-round of incarceration and freedom. Prison, however, provided de Sade time to write. His most depraved work, *The 120 Days of Sodom*, was composed on a forty-foot roll of paper inside the Bastille. In it, he chronicles the doings of a group of wealthy middle-aged men who spend the allotted 120 days in a castle abusing and killing a gaggle of victims, which includes various pubescent girls and boys, four old ladies, their own wives and daughters, and eight men chosen solely for the enormous size of their penises. It's worse than it sounds. A *lot* worse.

Donatien
Alphonse
François

de SADE

The French Revolution proved to be de Sade's lucky day; the new men in charge were far more accepting of his sexual escapades than the previous administration. In fact, not only did the marquis get released, but as Citizen Louis de Sade, he took an active role in local politics. Even for de Sade, though, the Reign of Terror was a bit over the top; he found himself again in jail, this time convicted, amazingly, of the crime of "moderatism." With the overthrow of Robespierre, de Sade was spared the guillotine and released, only to be tossed back into jail by Napoleon for his pornographic writings. Declared insane, de Sade was transferred to an asylum, where he began a paid affair with a chambermaid in her early teens that continued until he died in his sleep, peacefully.

The Marquis de Sade, by the way, was really fat.

shrap·nel *n. Fragments from an explosion.*
Henry Shrapnel was a lieutenant in the British Royal Artillery when, on his own initiative and dime, he developed an exploding cannonball. Originally dubbed "spherical case shot," the weapon came to be called the Shrapnel shell after its 1803 adoption by the British army. Jacques Chauvin and French soldiers everywhere just called it bad news, and in 1814 Shrapnel was awarded a lifetime twelve-hundred-pound-a-year pension for his contribution to the empire.

side·burns *n. The hair that grows on the side of the face in front of the ears.*

General Ambrose Burnside had about as bad a war as any general on the winning side can have. In the early days of the Civil War Burnside presided over the left wing of the Army of the Potomac at Antietam, where he failed to distinguish himself. Nevertheless, when Lincoln fired the overcautious General McClellan from overall command of the Union army, he promoted Burnside, who himself doubted he was up to the job. Burnside promptly led the North to its humiliating defeat at Fredericksburg and the even more humiliating "Mud March." Excoriated by his inferior officers, Burnside wanted them punished for insubordination and offered to resign if he was wrong. To Burnside's surprise, Lincoln accepted his resignation and awarded the job to the most vicious of his critics, General Joseph Hooker.

Burnside's Civil War career was not over, however, as he played a key role in what would become known as the Battle of the Crater. In an attempt to break the stalemate at the Siege of Petersburg, Union leadership devised a Secret Plan. The first part of the operation went wondrously well—coal miners dug a shaft under Confederate lines and detonated an enormous cache of dynamite, killing scores of Johnny Reb. But as Burnside's men were pursuing the fleeing Southern troops, the plan went awry. A division of black troops tapped to lead the charge around the edge of the

General
Ambrose
BURNSIDE

crater was pulled back, for fear of political repercussions if too many were killed (or so Grant later claimed). Unfamiliar with the plan, the replacement white soldiers decided, Wile E. Coyote–like, to take the most direct route across the battlefield: right *into* the crater. The Confederates reformed, circled the rim, and shot down Union troops like fish in a barrel. Burnside was finally, mercifully discharged, never to be recalled again.

And yes, he had facial hair. In fact, his sideburns were so long that they met each other via the mustache, a nineteenth-century fashion that has yet to come back into vogue. This muttonchops-to-mustache style was called the Burnside, or burnsides; at some point the word did a flip-flop, and sideburns receded from the nose until they stayed firmly hugging the ears, where they belong.

sil·hou·ette *n. A shape distinctly outlined by background.* While living in London, Étienne de Silhouette stumbled onto the black-magic secrets of Anglo-Saxon capitalism and fiscal responsibility. He returned to Paris spreading the dark gospel, no more popular on the Champs-Élysées in the mid-1700s than now. Silhouette, however, had the ear of the royal mistress, Madame de Pompadour, through whose devices he was elevated to be *Contrôleur général des finances*. To pay down the crushing debt being incurred from the ongoing Seven Years' War, Silhouette suggested what amounted to an import of the British Window Tax, although he wanted to tax doors too, and just about everything else he could think of. Silhouette also proposed slashing the pay of bureaucrats—again, never a way into the Gallic heart—and even ordered the king to melt down the royal plate.

The most amazing thing about Silhouette's departure after nine months in the office was that he lasted so long. Parisian ridicule of the finance minister didn't stop with his fall from grace, and anything made on the cheap was said to be done *à la silhouette*, including the then-popular method of producing a portrait without having to draw, in which the "artist" traced the subject's shadow onto a piece of black paper, cut it out, and stuck it in a frame.

so·lon *n. A wise and august legislator; generally used mockingly.*

Unable to live with the despised legal code of Draco, Athens voted to give another legislator dictatorial powers to correct it sometime around 593 B.C. As *Archon Eponymos** Solon imposed a basket of laws that would come to be regarded as the world's first constitution and earn Solon honor as one of the Seven Sages. Solon erased capital punishment for most crimes save murder and lessened legal distinctions between rich and poor. According to Draco's laws, a debtor who fell behind on payments became a serf or was forced into slavery, even if he was an honest farmer and Athenian citizen. Under Solon such persons were freed.

Solon is also said to have set up state-sponsored brothels, wanting to make sex "democratically" available to all. Not for nothing was he known as the people's champion.

While *draconian* has entered the wider vocabulary, *solon* is mostly relegated to wonky political reporting. Maybe that's because *draconian* is evocative of *dragon* and *Dracula*; when draconian action is taken, you know that's not a good thing. Plus, draconian just sounds cool. Solon, on the other hand, rhymes with colon.

---

*Archons were the magistrates of Athens, and the chief among them was the *Archon Eponymos*, so-called because the year in which he served was named after him.

THE ANCIENT WORD

The best and brightest of the ancient world live on in the English language. The term *epicurean* derives from the live-and-let-live theories of the philosopher Epicurus, while *platonic* of course comes from Plato, who began the first academy in a grove named after the mythic Athenian hero Academos. Thespis is said to have been a great actor who created masks with built-in megaphones so that even spectators in the nosebleeds could hear what the actors (or *thespians*) were saying onstage. Sapphic love is woman-on-woman love, after the great poetess Sappho, whose connection to that sexual orientation is so strong that we borrow not only her name to identify it but her birthplace, the island of Lesbos.

Then there are some less familiar words, for those who want to build their vocabulary, or already have one:

A philippic is a bitter tirade, usually condemning a particular individual. The original philippics took place in Athens and were made in denunciation of Philip II of Macedon (Alexander the Great's daddy) by Demosthenes, who argued that the foreign king was taking on too much power. He was right.

Mithridatism means to build up a tolerance to poison by taking gradual amounts of it (usually used metaphorically), a strategy employed by Mithridates the Great.

Mithridates aspired to an Alexander-like Hellenic empire, fighting—at times with remarkable success—the greatest Roman generals of his day, including Sulla, Lucullus, and Pompey. He failed.

A lucullan feast is over the top in lavish luxury and sumptuousness, like every meal Mithridates' foe Lucullus ever ate after returning from his great victories in the East. Cicero and Pompey were frequent party crashers.

A cicerone is a learned tour guide, after Cicero, the Roman senator renowned to be the greatest Latin orator of all time, but whose brilliant tongue caused his downfall. In the series of speeches he called the Phillipics (in reference to Demosthenes, thus coining the term), Cicero viciously attacked Mark Antony, the wrong man to piss off at the time. After Cicero's execution and dismemberment, Antony's wife stabbed Cicero's vaunted tongue over and over again with her hairpin, just in case he hadn't gotten the message.

spoon·er·ism *n. Swapping the beginning of words in speech, as in getting it bass ackwards.*

You may never have heard the term but you've surely made the mistake. Reverend William Archibald Spooner spent more than sixty years at Oxford as a student, teacher, and dean whose error-prone speaking style made for some pretty entertaining lectures.

"The Lord is a shoving leopard," he supposedly uttered in one class. Among his other alleged flubs are "It is kiss-tomary to cuss the bride," his telling a wayward student, "You've tasted two worms," and his famous toast, "Let us raise our glasses to our queer old dean!"

Small, pink-faced, and nearsighted, the beloved Spooner was the Mr. Magoo of Oxford, but he could get prickly about his odd fame. "You don't want a speech," he said to a group of clamoring students. "You only want me to say one of those . . . things." Unlike many of the other folks in this volume, Spooner eventually became a good sport about his eponymous fame, even if he maintained he only ever made his trademark mistake *once*.*

---

* "The Kinquering Congs Their Titles Take."

syph·i·lis *n. A type of venereal disease.*

Syphilus was a New World shepherd descended from the lost race of Atlantis who began losing his copious flock of beasts during a terrible drought. Cursing Apollo, Syphilus smashed the sun god's temples and started worshipping someone else. Miffed, Apollo struck the shepherd down with a horrendous new affliction.

> *He first wore buboes dreadful to the sight,*
> *First felt strange pains and sleepless passed the night;*
> *From him the malady received its name,*
> *The neighboring shepherds caught the spreading flame.*

Although you might think he's implying something with that last line about the amorous habits of shepherds, the author of the poem didn't even know that you caught the disease from sex. Girolamo Fracastoro of Verona was a Renaissance man's Renaissance man, a highly esteemed Latin poet, dabbler in astronomy (he and Copernicus were pals), and the greatest physician of his day. He had two goals with *Syphilis, or the French Disease*: one, to explore the nature of a dreaded malady, and two, to blame it all on the French.

Writing sixteen years later, Dottore Fracastoro used his fictional shepherd's name as the clinical term for the disease in his treatise *On Contagion and Contagious Diseases*. In this work, Fracastoro theorized that certain types of

Girolamo Fracastoro, author of
SYPHILIS

sickness were spread by tiny "seeds" traveling person-to-person through bodily contact, the air, or a contaminated intermediary. Although often hailed as the father of germ theory, Fracastoro had zero conception of microscopic organisms; rather, he thought these poisonous seeds resulted from a bum planetary alignment of Saturn, Jupiter, and Mars. Still, his description of how infectious diseases traveled represented an advancement in the field of medicine.

tan·ta·lize *v. To tempt with the unattainable.*

Tantalus was one of Zeus's many half-mortal progeny, and his worst-behaved. Invited to Olympus for a feast of the gods, Tantalus embarrassed his dad by stealing nectar and ambrosia from the table and smuggling it back down to the mortal plane to share with his fellow nondeities. This crime cost him big-time in the afterlife. Tantalus was banished to Tartarus, the deepest part of the underworld, and forced to stand in a river up to his chin surrounded by trees full of ripe, low-hanging fruit. If he tried to drink, the water would flow faster and dip, and if he reached for the fruit, wind would draw the branches up out of his grasp.

Forever.

taw·dry *adj. Slutty, in a cheap and sordid way.*

Once upon a time (the middle of the seventh century), there was a young English princess named Æthelthryth, or, as the Normans would later call her, Audrey. Princess Audrey was widowed after a marriage that, we are told, was never consummated. She took a vow of chastity but her father the king required that Audrey marry again; her new hubby, understandably less than thrilled about her promise to God, bribed the local bishop to make the vow go away. The bishop instead helped Audrey escape, but hubby got wise and gave chase. Divine intervention in the form of a prolonged high tide provided Audrey cover for her getaway, causing her husband to give up and find himself a more ready gal to marry. Becoming a nun, Audrey founded the Abbey of Ely. Many years later, as she lay dying after a life of good works, Audrey developed a red, burning tumor around her neck, which she gladly accepted as just punishment for the many frivolous necklaces she had worn in her youth. As a reward for Audrey's extreme devotion to not having sex, she was sainted, and her feast day was celebrated with an annual fair held at Ely.

In a show of medieval irony, a certain kind of frilly silk neckerchief was known as the lace of Saint Audrey, or "Taudrey Lace." This item was a top seller at the Taudrey fair, especially amongst "country wenches" who bought the cheapest and gaudiest varieties, paying little heed to Audrey's cautionary neck-tumor-for-necklace tale.

As for how *Audrey* got to be *tawdry*, similar contractions happen with 'twere, 'tis, and another initial-A saint, Anthony, in the archaic terms *tantony bell*, *tantony crutch*, and *tantony pig*. Saint Anthony was the patron saint of swineherds, and the tantony was the runt of the litter; *tantony* came figuratively to mean one who follows too close behind, as in, *Don't tantony me!*

BANTERS AND BOBBIES

Slang is the most significant divider between the Englishes spoken on the opposing shores of the Atlantic, as well as the main vehicle by which names move into words, so it's no surprise John Bull's English has a few anonyponyms obscure to the Yankee ear.

A *mackintosh* is a raincoat, named after the Scotsman who first successfully marketed the stuff it was made out of. In 1823 Charles Macintosh patented a material made out of India rubber and naphtha, a tar by-product, with the purpose of creating waterproof clothing. A mackintosh is now more commonly called a mac, and in either form it has become slang for a condom.

Titchy means something really small, as in tiny, and derives from Little Tich, the stage name of Harry Relph, a fourish-foot-tall English music-hall comedian famed for his "Big Boot" dance, performed in twenty-eight-inch-long shoes. His nickname "Tich," however, came from the Tichborne claimant, a man who in 1866 convinced the mother of Sir Roger Charles Doughty Tichborne that he was the son she had lost to the sea twelve years earlier, never mind that he had put on a couple hundred pounds, changed hair color, and mysteriously lost the ability to speak French. The Tichborne scandal filled London papers for a decade, until the claimant—real name Arthur Orton, formerly a butcher from Wagga Wagga, Australia—was convicted of perjury and sentenced to fourteen years' hard labor. Relph, a pudgy young child at the time of the trial, was called Tich for his resemblance to the enormously obese Orton.

In 1829, Home Secretary Robert Peel established the first police force in London—one of the first such groups in the world—and made further history by choosing Scotland Yard as its base of operations. Peel had begun his law-enforcement career in Ireland, where he organized the Royal Irish Constabulary (later muscle for the potato-picking scabs of Charles Boycott), earning him the nickname "Orange Peel." His foot soldiers were known derisively as *peelers*, a term adopted by Londoners, who also called the policemen *bobbies*.

Unpopular though they may have been, Bobby's boys proved hugely effective, helping to launch a political career that saw Peel get elected prime minister twice before coming to grief over the Potato Famine.

While the Irish were starving, the English were getting fat. In 1863, an undertaker and carpenter named William Banting wrote *A Letter on Corpulence Addressed to the Public* in which he outlined how he had lost fifty pounds in no time at all while eating an extra meal a day and not exercising. He did this by forsaking carbs and sugar; in other words, he did the Atkins diet a hundred years before Dr. Atkins created it. Banting's self-published pamphlet swiftly became an international phenomenon, finding a success that eluded his American forebear, Dr. Graham. Unlike the Graham diet, however, no religious angle existed in Banting's—it was just about getting skinnier. "Do you *bant*?" became the question everyone asked each other, at least among the bourgeois set. The verb, sadly, is obsolete today even in British English, though not quite obsolete all together (see p. 135).

Tues·day *n. The third day of the week, and usually the most boring.*

Have you ever wondered how we got the *Tues-* in Tuesday? When Germanic types adopted the Roman week (see p. 55), they decided to make some changes. *Sun-day* and *Moon-day* they translated without prejudice, but for the rest of the week the Teutons wanted their own gods watching over them, and so instead of having the days of Mars, Mercury, Jove, and Venus, they created Tiw's day, Woden's day, Thor's day, and Frig's day. (For some unknown reason, the Teutons had no problem with Saturn and let him have his day, which is ironic, since in Romance languages Saturn was the one god's name *not* kept; instead, most adopted some form of the Hebrew word *sabbath*.)

Woden/Wotan and Frig/Fricka will be familiar to lovers of Wagner, as will Thor to aficionados of Stan Lee and Jack Kirby; but who on earth was Tiw? Although god of martial glory (which is why he replaced Mars), Tiw had a rather unfortunate incident with Fenrir, an apocalyptically dangerous wolf. Fenrir broke every shackle put upon him, so the gods of Asgard called upon the dwarves of Svartálfaheim to devise a magic ribbon that was thin as silk, light as air, and unbreakable, which the little fellows fabricated from the breath of fish, a woman's beard, the sound of a cat's footsteps, and a few of their other favorite things, none of which exist any longer as a result.

"You'd sure look good in this ribbon," the gods all told Fenrir, but the wolf, sensing a trap, said he'd only try it on if Tiw held his hand hostage in the wolf's mouth. Tiw, brave, honest, and not all that smart, did as the wolf requested. Once the ribbon was on, Fenrir was trapped, and the gods all laughed and kept laughing, even when Fenrir bit Tiw's hand off. In light of his good faith, Tiw was made the god of oaths, treaties, and contracts. He also became known, aptly enough, as the one-handed god.

tup·per·ware *n. A reusable plastic storage container.*
Pedestrian though they seem today, the idea of plastic food containers was so revolutionary in the late 1940s that inventor Earl Tupper had a heck of a time selling them. His patented "burping seal"—that guarantee of freshness—baffled consumers. Mr. Tupper's product might never have taken off if not for Brownie Wise, a preternaturally well-named single mother from Detroit who started selling Tupperware at social gatherings and soon was encouraging other women to follow her example. So successful was Wise that in 1951 Tupper pulled his product out of stores and put all sales directly into her hands.

Although today thought of as a quaint relic of the preliberated housewife, the Tupperware party was in fact a progressive step, as all over America (and soon the world) housewives got a taste of entrepreneurship and cold, hard cash. Selling Tupperware was about making money, and more: Wise was a female Norman Vincent Peale who dared women to dream and offered them the "suffrage of success." She herself took to that freedom with glad alacrity, tooling around in a pink Cadillac and becoming the first woman to appear on the cover of *Business Week*. Jealous of her fame, Tupper fired her. Shortly thereafter, the inventor divorced his wife, sold his company for sixteen million dollars, gave up his U.S. citizenship for tax purposes, and moved to Costa Rica, where he would die in obscurity.

ves·pas·ian *n. A kind of public urinal found on the streets of Latin-speaking countries. Literally, on the streets.*
A man like Vespasian might have been remembered for lots of things: the construction of the Colosseum, the put-down of revolts in the Judea, the conquering of new lands in Britain. Instead, the name of this first-century Roman emperor will forever be connected with the Urine Tax.

Coming out the victor in the Year of the Four Emperors (as chaotic a time as its name implies), Vespasian was faced with some serious budget shortfalls. One major untaxed natural resource was urine. Cleaners needed fermented urine—ammonia—in order to keep their customers' togas a sparkling white, so they posted buckets outside their doors into which passersby could relieve themselves. Knowing a golden revenue stream when he saw one, Vespasian taxed the cleaners on the piss they collected. When the emperor's son Titus told his father he found the tax repulsive, the old man held out a gold coin for Titus to sniff and said, "Money don't stink."

volt·age *n. An amount of energy, often figurative.*
Born and raised in the idyllic lakeside city of Como, Alessandro Volta began his career as a high school physics teacher with a passion for electricity. His first advances were made in developing the electrophorus, a device that produced a static electric charge, and he also liked to play around with exploding gases (his favorite being methane, which he is credited with "discovering"). Investigating the work of Galvani and his famous frog, Volta rejected his colleague's theory of animal electricity and countered what he termed "galvanism" with his own theory that electric current was produced by the contact of two different metals. Upon this principle, Volta developed the world's first battery in 1800. The following year, he demonstrated his invention to Napoleon, who rewarded Volta by making him a count.

Between them, Volta and Galvani did more than anyone else to usher in the age of electricity, and left their mark

Count Alessandro VOLTA

not only on science and language but also literature: It was after discussing galvanism that Mary Shelley came up with the idea for *Frankenstein*.

wimp *n. A wuss.*

The original wimp was J. Wellington Wimpy, the porkpie-hatted mooch of the Popeye cartoons, whose perennial gambit "I would gladly pay you Tuesday for a hamburger today" never quite succeeded.

E. C. Segar's *Thimble Theatre*, the comic strip in which Popeye first appeared, is remarkable for its contribution to the lexicon. In addition to *wimp*, Segar is also responsible for the word *goon*, from his hairy warrior woman Alice the Goon, and probably the vehicle name *Jeep*, after Olive Oyl's pet Eugene the Jeep, a magical and resourceful creature from the fourth dimension whose entire vocabulary consisted of the single word "Jeep!"

zep·pe·lin *n. A dirigible airship; best when not filled with hydrogen.*

Count Ferdinand von Zeppelin caught the aviation bug when he was a military observer attached to the Union Army Balloon Corps. The chief mission of President Lincoln's aeronauts was to provide reconnaissance, but von Zeppelin came away convinced that aircraft could do more, provided they became engine-powered and steerable. His answer was a motor-powered balloon with a hard shell, called a dirigible (as opposed to a nonrigid airship, or blimp). Von Zeppelin's first successful flight didn't come until 1900, but just nine years later the count produced a model that reached speeds of fifty miles per hour and would go on to stock the fleet of DELAG, the world's first commercial airline.

Zeppelins were soon carrying out air-raid missions—another first—but their success in such capacity was short-lived once the getting-bombed-upon Brits realized that dirigibles were just big balloons waiting to be popped by gunfire. The postwar era would prove the golden age of the zeppelin, as airships competed with ocean liners for the transatlantic passenger business, matching them in luxury and, flying at a pleasant low distance above the ground, offering the advantage of sightseeing. Zeppelin routes went as far afield from Germany as Brazil, and the spire of the Empire State Building was designed to moor dirigibles.

Count Ferdinand
von ZEPPELIN

(The 102nd floor was to be the landing platform, but it didn't work.)

The death of the zeppelin came with the spectacular 1937 Hindenburg disaster that took place over Lakehurst, New Jersey. The Nazis were using zeppelins for propaganda (much as Goodyear would in later years), but they had no access to helium; only the U.S. possessed the gas in industrial quantities, and they weren't selling, at least not to Hitler. Some *dummkopf* decided to fill the eight-hundred-foot-long Hindenburg with the highly flammable gas hydrogen, and the rest, as they say, is history.

ANONYPONYMS
SANS FRONTIÈRES

A zeppelin is a zeppelin in languages across the world, except when it's not. The standard term is often some form of the word *dirigible*. A reverse situation holds for the airship's aimless cousin: What we call a hot-air balloon is known in other countries for the French brothers who invented it.

Although an American education might have you believe that the first men to fly were the Wright brothers, another pair of brothers beat them to the punch—by 120 years. Joseph and Jacques Montgolfier created the vehicle that produced the first manned flight in 1783, a balloon given lift by what the brothers called Montgolfier Gas. (It was just plain air, lest you think they produced gas in some other manner.) Their first flight crew consisted of a duck, a rooster, and a sheep; seeing their barnyard trio survive, the brothers sent humans skyward. Their creation is known as a *montgolfier* in French and a *montgolfiere* in Italian.

Trademarked names have taken root in languages everywhere, but even with global brands acceptance varies from country to country. You can take a *yacuzzi* in Spain or a *jacuzzibad* in Sweden, but in Portugal and Germany you'll have to settle for a *banho de hidromassagem* and a *Sprudelbad*. A ballpoint pen is a *biro* in many parts of the world (Britain and Australia included), for its inventor László Biró, or a *bic*, after Marcel Bich, a Frenchman who licensed the technology from the Hungarian Biró. (Monsieur Bich was afraid his name would be mispronounced *Bitch* in anglophone countries, hence the spelling change.)

The eponyms used most widely and consistently come from the international world of science. A volt is a volt wherever you go, as are the psychological conditions of masochism and sadism (more or less). There's a division, however, with *X-ray*. The Romance languages are in sync with the English formulation (e.g., the Spanish *rayos X*), which was coined by the discoverer of the X-ray, Wilhelm Röntgen, who in 1895 took the first X-ray photograph. (It was of his wife's hand.) His native tongue, however, ditched the doctor's suggestion and chose instead to honor Wilhelm himself, and so an X-ray is a *Roentgen* in German, as it is in most languages across northern and central Europe.

Medical terms tend to get discarded once the theories behind them have been discredited, as in the English-speaking world with *onanism* and the implication that masturbation is a wasting affliction. It remains standard usage, however, in countries such as Sweden (*onani*) and Germany (*Onanie*).

More resilient have been certain political anonyponyms that spread like wildfire because they so captured a moment and continue to be relevant today. People around the globe have no more idea of who Charles Boycott was than English speakers do, but what's striking about his word is the level of adoption it achieved, and how swiftly. Less than fifty years after the first boycott, the government of propagandist

boycot	Dutch
Boykott	German
boykot	Filipino, Danish, Turkish
bojkot	Czech, Polish, Serbian, Slovenian
bojkott	Hungarian, Swedish
bojkotim	Albanian
бойкот	Bulgarian, Russian
boikot	Indonesian
boikott	Estonian, Norwegian
boikotti	Finnish
boikotto	Japanese
boikotas	Lithuanian
boikots	Latvian
boicot	Catalan, Romanian, Spanish
boicote	Portuguese
boycottage	French
boicottaggio	Italian

extraordinaire Benito Mussolini launched a political campaign to banish all nonnative words—*le parole stranieri*—from the Italian vocabulary. For example, a *croissant* by law had to be called a *bombola*. And the slogan on posters? ITALIANI, BOICOTTARE LE PAROLE STRANIERI!

Another political eponym, *chauvinism*, became useful in the face of nationalist movements that upended the world in war and strife—and found itself transformed into

Polish *szowinizm*, Czech *šovinizmus*, Indonesian *sovinisme*, and Filipino *tsowinisma*, to name a few. It should be noted that the sexist connotation English chauvinism has taken on is missing in other languages. The Italian *sciovinismo* refers to excessive patriotism or partisanship, while what we would call male chauvinism is there styled *maschilismo* (formed in opposition, naturally, to *femminismo*). To mesmerize means to spellbind in English, but in other tongues remains a synonym for *hypnotize*, or is relegated specifically to the practices of Franz Mesmer. Sometimes figurative meanings wander quite far afield. A judas is a traitor in many languages, but in French it refers to a peephole, betrayer of the person being spied upon.

Literary eponyms are less likely than others to cross borders, excepting those based on widespread classics such as *Don Quixote*, attested to by English *quixotic*, Spanish *quijotesco*, and the arabesque Italian adverb *donchisciottescamente*. (In Italian, Cervantes's work is *Don Chisciotte* [key-SHOAT-tay], if that helps parse it.) As for a word from an English book, *lolita* is spreading fast, more so in other languages than in the one it was written in. Generally it means a sexually precocious or aggressive young girl, although in Japan the word has come to represent a goth fashion style.

Ludwig Bemelmans's 1941 travel book *The Donkey Inside* produced a word unique to the Spanish of Ecuador, *bemelmans*, which means "foreigner who makes fun of natives." A sampling of text that might have offended: "We have a revolution here every Thursday at half-past two, and our government is run like a nightclub."

A number of people live on in other languages but not their own. *Martinet* as an eponym does not exist in the drillmaster's native tongue, although French has a word *chatterton* that means electrical tape after its British inventor, while *bant* endures in Swedish as the word for dieting. And though Pullman (after George, developer of the sleeper car) has faded from the English vocabulary along with the tendency to take overnight train rides, *pullman* (pronounced POOL-mahn) has spread to become the general Italian word for bus.

I'd like to end our linguistic tour by nominating a particularly handy word for English-language adoption. Johann Ballhorn, a printer during the last quarter of the sixteenth century, was responsible for publishing an important law book for his home city of Luebeck. In the process of correcting an earlier edition—a typical task of the printer in those days—Ballhorn wound up making mistakes where none had earlier been, thereby causing a legacy of legal disputes and bequeathing to German a verb, *verballhornen*, "to make worse through correcting."

EPONYM WATCH LIST

Most eponyms die. Few outlive the fame of the people who birthed them, and most fade even faster. Some are superseded by synonyms while others become technologically obsolete, as is the case with the *brougham*, *hansom*, and *phaeton*, three types of horse carriages named after a couple of Englishmen and a kid who wrecked his father's wheels. Fiction-based eponyms depend largely upon the vagaries of literary taste. In this respect no one has suffered more than Charles Dickens, once the most widely read writer in the English language, now falling off reading lists everywhere. A *scrooge* is known to all and a *fagin* understood by many, but who still knows what *gamp*, *pecksniffian*, or *gradgrind* mean? (If you want to be the one, they are: an umbrella, after Sarah Gamp of *Martin Chuzzlewit*; hypocritical, for Seth Pecksniff of same; and a man given to facts, such as Thomas Gradgrind in *Hard Times*.)

Below find some eponyms lamentably lost or seriously imperiled. Language is what its speakers make it, so you have power to revive them.

annie oakley
Annie Oakley, the sharpshooting star of Buffalo Bill's Wild West show, had her own breed of card tricks. At a distance of thirty paces, she could shoot out the heart in the ace of hearts, split a playing card in half with a bullet edgeways, and shoot half a dozen holes into a card tossed into the air before it hit the ground. Her name came to mean a free ticket or pass, as in one that's already been punched.
Status: defunct

baedeker
A guidebook, after the widely read publications of Karl Baedeker, whose company started producing travel manuals in 1827. The "Baedeker raids" of World War II were so-called because the Germans struck at historical sites featured in *Baedeker's Great Britain*.
Status: faint pulse

give a bell
Alexander Graham Bell was literally an eponym machine, bequeathing Ma Bell, the Baby Bells, decibel, and this term, for calling someone on the phone.
Status: under revival

bogart
Humphrey Bogart has the distinction of *two* English verbs springing from his surname. The first means to act like a tough guy or intimidate, as in, "Don't bogart your little brother."
Status: died out a generation ago

 The second verb, meaning to steal something in small increments, went mainstream in the sixties time-capsule

movie *Easy Rider*. "Don't bogart that joint, my friend..."
begins the chorus of the song playing while Jack Nicholson
rides on the back of Peter Fonda's chopper. Its extended
sense of "to be greedily protective of something" has lately
been moving the verb out of its cannabis pigeonhole, which
speaks well for its prospects for long-term survival (as does the
fact that most people using it have never seen the Humphrey
Bogart smokefest known as *Casablanca*).
Status: burgeoning

pull a brodie
To commit suicide, usually figuratively, coined in 1886 after
Steve Brodie jumped off the Brooklyn Bridge to win a bet and
survived. Although his feat was considered by many a hoax,
Brodie parlayed his fame into a touristy saloon on the Bowery
and acting gigs in a couple of vaudeville shows. He was later
portrayed in the movies by George Raft and served as Bugs
Bunny's foil in "Bowery Bugs." (Out of sheer exasperation with
the rabbit, he jumps off the bridge again at the end.)
Status: jumped the shark long ago

burke
When an old man died owing back rent at his Edinburgh
boarding house, landlord William Hare hit upon a unique way
of getting the money out of him: selling the deadbeat's corpse.
With his friend William Burke, Hare stole the body out of its
coffin and brought it to the local anatomy school. Seeing how
well it paid, the duo entered into the dissection-supply business. Turning the lodging house into an operation Procrustes
would have admired, Hare and Burke murdered at least fifteen
transients before getting caught Halloween night, 1828. The

evidence was circumstantial, but in turn for immunity Hare confessed, which is why he walked free and his pal got hanged, and the verb meaning "to smother to death or hush up" is to *burke* and not to *hare*.

Status: worth reviving

not to be grahamed

Giuseppe Mazzini was the intellectual father of the Risorgimento, the Italian unification movement. A philosopher and agitator with a death sentence hanging over his head, in 1837 Mazzini settled in London, a city that prided itself for its fair treatment of political exiles. When the British government was discovered to be opening Mazzini's mail, the scandal was blamed on Home Secretary James Graham, and Britons began writing NOT TO BE GRAHAMED on their envelopes in elegant protest.

Status: extinct

lindbergh it

To go solo, as in out to dinner, or wherever.

Status: my mother still uses it

lucy stoner

A slur targeting a woman who doesn't take her husband's name, coined after the marriage of suffragette Lucy Stoner in 1855. The surname Ms. Stoner chose not to take: Blackwell.

Status: historical use only

mae west

An inflatable life preserver. Get it?

Status: deckside humor on senior cruises

mickey

As in, to be slipped a mickey, or—to use the full expression—a Mickey Finn, meaning a drink that's been laced with a knockout drug or hallucinogen; by extension, a real strong drink. The original Mickey Finn owned the Lone Star Saloon in turn-of-the-century Chicago; he would rather ungraciously sedate his customers in the aforementioned manner, rob them, and dump their unconscious bodies in an alley (but hey, at least he didn't burke them). The saloon was shut down and Finn convicted in 1903, done in by the testimony of his accomplices, "house girls" Isabelle Fyffe and Mary "Gold Tooth" Thornton.
Status: annoying hipster use

milquetoast

Caspar Milquetoast was everything you might expect from the protagonist of a comic strip entitled *Timid Soul*, created in 1924 by H. T. Webster.
Status: dated

pinchbeck

Counterfeit, false, cheap, worthless, tawdry. Christopher Pinchbeck was a London watchmaker in the early 1700s who marketed jewelry made out of imitation gold, the alloy of which (lots of copper and a bit of zinc) he developed himself.
Status: used in intellectually elitist periodicals

AFTERWORD

When I was little, my mother told me that the word *pumper-nickel* came from the name of Napoleon's horse, Nickel. While encamped in Germany, Napoleon's soldiers complained about the indigestible local black bread. Napoleon responded that his horse liked the stuff well enough. "If it's *bon pour Nickel*," the little Corsican said, "then it's good for you too."

Sadly, the tale is utterly apocryphal. The origin for the name likely comes from *pumper*, a German word meaning "fart." It is one of many enticing word stories I would have loved to include in the book but couldn't.

People have postulated that the term *jerry-built* refers to the handiwork of a Jerry Bros. construction firm that put up exceptionally shoddy housing in late-1800s London, but they offer no proof. Eponym hunters have also searched the world for the first person to be *batty* and turned up two plausible candidates: one, Jamaican barrister Fitzherbert Batty, declared legally insane in the 1800s; and two, William Battie, eighteenth-century author of *A Treatise on Madness*. So which is the right one? Neither. The word derives from the phrase "bats in the belfry."

Historians have cried eponymy to discredit subjects they don't like. In his work of the 1570s, *Perambulation of Kent*, William Lambarde wrote that the first *harlot* was Arlette, mother of William the Conqueror, known to chauvinistic Englishmen as William the Bastard. Lambarde was nursing a grudge over the 1066 Norman invasion but most probably believed the etymology; certainly it has been cited countless times in the four centuries since. However, to look at a passage from Chaucer—"A sturdy harlot went them aye behind, / That was their hoste's man, and bare a sack, / And what men gave them, laid it on his back"—we see that the word previously meant a different kind of worker.

At least *harlot* has a reasonable false etymology; other would-be eponyms are plain silly. *Condom* has been said to derive from either a Dr. Condom, personal physician to King Charles II of England, or the Earl of Condom. There is no Condom in Britain to be an Earl of, nor is Condom a known English surname, although Condon is, which is how the prophylactic was sometimes spelt in the 1700s. But in the earliest extant reference the spelling is *quondam*, leading to the suggestion that it is derived from the Italian word *guantone*, which roughly translates to "a big glove." In short, the etymology is unknown, but hope remains alive that we will find a lusty but careful Mr. Condon out there.

Great long lists of eponyms can be found all over the Internet, some so loaded with counterfeits that more than half the names are phonies. But even one conscientious site has, among hundreds of accurate entries, the apocryphal figures Nathaniel Bigot (said to have been an English Puritan teacher), a Portuguese man named João Marmalado, and Leopold von Asphalt.

My favorite fraud is the esteemed Dominican scholar Domenico da Comma (1260–1316). This Italian monk inserted his namesake commas into the heretofore woefully under-punctuated Bible to make it more readily comprehensible. For his efforts, da Comma was charged with heresy by the Inquisition, who considered his editorial improvement "an affront to God." If only it were so; the word instead comes from the Greek *komma*, cut off.

But things are not always so clear, nor is it only the Internet that gets things wrong. Was Nicholas Chauvin a real person? No one knows, but he is almost always cited as such. Thomas Crapper is often thought to belong on da Comma's list because of a comically grand pseudobiography, *Flushed with Pride*, that made him seem entirely made-up. More often than whether a person existed, however, the question is whether we've found the right one. For *lynch*, different reference works definitively support Charles (*Encyclopaedia Britannica*) and William (*Oxford English Dictionary*).

Then there's the question of whether a word is an eponym at all, which often comes down to a matter of personal preju-dice. Killjoy etymologists cite antebellum uses of the word *hooker* in the sense of "prostitute" as gotcha-game proof that the word is noneponymous. But without Hooker's Division would the term have endured? Lord knows we have enough synonyms to get by. All words—and proper names are words— go back to some earlier word, so to put too much weight on the "original" source is to be simplistic.

Even when eponymy is certain, much else is not. Myths inevitably pop up to fashion people with more direct roles in the creation of what bears their name: The derby was first worn by the Earl of Derby to his horse race (false); Silhouette practiced the art of shade cutting (seems unlikely); Cardigan invented the sweater he and his men wore into battle (almost assuredly not); Saint Audrey had a neck tumor, which is why a gaudy neckerchief was named after her (surprisingly true, or the Venerable Bede is a liar).

In many cases, the legend itself is what's important. Whether or not Chauvin existed is meaningless for its development as a word. This is true of more than folklore; historians gossip, too, and not just William Batarde. Wanting to show the Bourbon kings to be spineless creatures controlled by their mistresses, nineteenth-century historians inflated Madame de Pompadour's role in national affairs. In the matter of her enduring fame, the myth of La Pompadour is at least as significant as the woman born Jeanne Antoinette Poisson.

While the power of popular perception is important, I put nothing in this book that to my better knowledge wasn't true, with one exception: the tale of our old friend, the Earl of Sandwich.

The mythology of the earl inventing sandwiches to get through a daylong gambling binge seems to have formed around a single source. It appeared in a travel book on London written by a visiting Frenchman who was repeating something juicy he had heard about one of the king's ministers. There's no corroborating evidence that the earl was a gambler of any sort; rather, he was said to be a tireless worker, leading to the conjecture that maybe he loved his sandwiches because they allowed him to *work* through the night, a claim proposed by his biographer and supported by his descendants (owners of the Earl of Sandwich restaurant chain), which seems only slightly less ridiculous than the Frenchman's tale.

In either event, what does it matter? It's just a macguffin.

NOTES

3 Philadelphia whiskey maker E.G. Booz: His product was memorably packaged in a log-cabin-shaped brown bottle; *to bouse* as a verb goes back to Middle English.

7 *algorithm* . . . Algorismus: The term *algorithm* developed after *algorism* (the original English word) got confused with *arithmos*, the Greek word for number.

10 scientific pig Latin: The naming system Linnaeus developed, set forth in his *Species plantarum* (1753) and *Systema naturae* (1758, tenth edition), includes a generic (genus) name and specific (species).

14 nearly thirty times what they were worth: The harvest reportedly cost the British government £10,000 for £350 worth of potatoes. "Boycott's legacy; Making a name for himself: British land agent Captain Charles Boycott was ostracised by the Irish." *Daily Mail* (September 27, 2007).

18 Improving upon Jackson's idea: Kellogg got his original start in the cereal business producing his own version of Granula, called Granula. Upon Jackson's apparent threat to sue, Kellogg renamed his product Granola. A former patient at John's sanitarium named C.W. Post then ripped off *Kellogg's* Granola recipe, creating Grape Nuts. Years later, hippies would revive the name of Kellogg's by-then defunct product for a new take on the cereal genre.

24 brought back home with them a new word: That, at least, is one theory, based on chronology and geography. To wit: Crapper went into business

in 1861; the OED cites "crapping ken" (1846), "crapping case" (1859), and "crapping-castle" (1874) as referring to outhouses and water closets, but *crapper* is first seen in American slang from the 1920s. The link from Thomas Crapper to the Americanism, if real, is yet to be discovered.

40 "That will do for a salamander!": A salamander is a variety of amphibian, but was long the name for a mythological, lizardlike creature that lived in fire and was closely related to the dragon. On Elkanah Tisdale's original drawing of the gerrymander, notice the silhouette of Governor Gerry under the beast's wing.

41 the lexical contributions: The term *superman* itself is not originally an eponym, but was coined by Friedrich Nietzsche (or, rather, his translators). Still, it's safe to posit that when someone says "Don't try to be a superman," they aren't talking about the proto-Nazi übermensch but rather the creation of Jerry Siegel and Joe Shuster, a couple of nice Jewish boys from Cleveland.

41 an amalgam of *brain* and *maniac*: The famed supercomputer ENIAC (Electronic Numerical Integrator and Automatic Calculator), built in 1946, also may have influenced the character's name.

41 Bizarro: The word *bizarre* may come from the language linguists consider the bizarro world, Basque, where the word *bizzara* means "beard."

43 *one Scuttled Butt*: A scuttlebutt was the deckside equivalent of the water cooler, literally and figuratively. Vernon's order appears in Michael Quinion's essay on grog ("World Wide Words: Grog," World Wide Words, www.worldwidewords.org/qa/qa-gro4.htm), as well as in Peter D. Jeans, *Seafaring Lore and Legend: A Miscellany of Maritime Myth, Superstition, Fable, and Fact* (McGraw-Hill Professional, 2004): 101–102.

43 "Old Grog": Grogram, from French *gros grain*, is a coarse fabric out of which were made cloaks and coats, often themselves called "grograms" by synecdoche. Vernon's ever-present grogram earned him the nickname Old Grog.

44 adopted, with vigor: Though often credited with the invention of the guillotine, Joseph-Ignace only proposed the device; its roots are centuries older. The version used in Revolutionary France was designed by Dr. Antoine Louis (who would die by one) and built by German harpsichord maker Tobias Schmidt. It quickly took on innumerable nicknames, among them the Louisette, the Louison, the widow, the national razor, the Capetian necktie, Guillotin's daughter, Mlle. Guillotin, and, of course, the guillotine. Supposedly, the Guillotin family lobbied to change the name of the device and, that failing, changed their own.

53 "bar-room and brothel": A grandson and great-grandson of presidents, Charles Francis Adams Jr. described Hooker's headquarters as "a place where no self-respecting man liked to go, and no decent woman could go . . . a combination of bar-room and brothel." Hugh Rawson, "Why Do We Say That?" *American Heritage* (Feb./March 2006): 16.

53 Hooker ordered that prostitutes: According to Thomas Power Lowry, *The Story the Soldiers Wouldn't Tell* (Mechanicsburg, PA: Stackpole Books, 1994): 64, "To aid the military police by localizing the problem, Hooker herded many of the prostitutes into the Murder Bay (future Federal Triangle) area."

53 regional slang term: Three antebellum citations have so far been found for *hooker*, two of which independently ascribe its origin to Corlear's Hook, a bawdy part of New York filled with sailors and brothels. Some think the word evolved from an earlier sense of *hooker* as a pickpocket, or the idea of a prostitute trying to "hook" a client. Likely, it was some combination of these elements, and the use of *hooker* formed a double or triple entendre — one of the entendres being Fighting Joe.

54 Patrick Hooligan: In 1898, tales of "Hooligan" gangs began appearing in London newspapers. A variation on the more familiar Houlihan, *hooligan* almost certainly derives from someone's name, but whose is in dispute. The main evidence for Patrick comes from Clarence Rook's *The Hooligan Nights* (New York: Henry Holt and Co., 1899), which recounts his story as told by patrons of the Lamb and Flag, a pub Hooligan frequented.

58 it kind of sounded African: A variety of African connections have been suggested, including a link to the Swahili word *jumbe*, or chief, and a possible connection to the West African bogeyman Mumbo Jumbo. According to the writer Jan Bondeson, the London Zoo superintendent who named

Jumbo also later named an African gorilla Mumbo. *The Feejee Mermaid and Other Essays in Natural and Unnatural History.* (Ithaca, NY: Cornell University Press, 1999): 99.

61 "The Daring Young Man on the Flying Trapeze": Composed in 1867, with words by Gaston Lyle and music by George Leybourne. From Howard Loxton, *The Golden Age of the Circus*, (New York: Smithmark Publishers, 1997): 68:

> *He flew through the air, with the greatest of ease*
> *This daring young man on the flying trapeze;*
> *His movements so graceful, all girls he could please*
> *And my love he purloined away.*

61 poor Jules died at thirty-one: The year of Léotard's birth, and his age at death, are in dispute. While many sources agree that he was born August 1, 1838, the years 1842 and 1839 have also been suggested. He died in 1870.

63 So which Lynch was it?: Charles was long considered the real Lynch, then the pendulum swung to William and has only in the last couple of years swung back to Charles. Much about the William thesis is easy to dismiss, since it rests on documents published long after the term entered the language (an 1811 account of Lynch's confession to South Carolina diarist Andrew Ellicott, an 1836 article in the *Southern Literary Messenger*, and a May 1859 article in *Harper's* magazine). Christopher Waldrep has provided essential research bolstering the Charles thesis, and was the source for much of this entry. See Christopher Waldrep, *The Many Faces of Judge Lynch: Extralegal Violence and Punishment in America* (New York: Palgrave Macmillan, 2002), and *Lynching in America: A History in Documents* (New York: New York University Press, 2006).

63 a hoax perpetrated by Edgar Allan Poe: Poe loved hoaxes, especially those he managed to get published in the newspaper. In 1844, he persuaded the *New York Sun* to publish an entirely false account of a European who had managed to cross the Atlantic in three days in a hot-air balloon.

64 The Milliner's Trade: The term milliner derives from those famed pliers of fancy wares (originally not just hats) of Milan.

64 the Southwark hatters who manufactured it: Other versions of the story say the name derives from the hatter John Bowler, and that it wasn't William who ordered the hat but a relation, Edward Coke.

66 Alexander Pope's *Dunciad*: The *Dunciad*, first published in 1728, was an epic parody in which Pope eviscerated many of his fellow authors of the day, whom he fashioned "dunces" living in the kingdom of Dulnes. By that time a dunce meant a general blockhead, though according to the Oxford English Dictionary Pope was also using the term with the special sense of one who has been made stupider by learning.

67 *sark*: *Sark* is cognate with the second half of *berserk*, Icelandic for bear-shirt, the dressing preference of some particularly bloodthirsty Viking warriors. *Cutty Sark* became the name of a nineteenth-century clipper ship that in turn inspired a brand of whisky.

71 slave signed the document "Dr. Leopold, Knight of Sacher-Masoch": Leopold von Sacher-Masoch, *Venus in Furs*. Trans. Jean McNeil, in *Masochism: Coldness and Cruelty & Venus in Furs* (New York: Zone Books, 1991): 278–279.

78 trance states: Mesmer was hypnotizing people without knowing it and "curing" them via hypnotic suggestion. He was no charlatan; he wanted badly to be investigated, believing he had made great scientific break-throughs. Since the Mesmer commission, faith healing has been shown to be effective, while energy flow and magnet wearing (both with long histo-ries pre-Mesmer) are back in vogue.

78 ironically for the monarch: Destined to die on Guillotin's machine along with the king was his wife, Marie Antoinette (a client of Mesmer's), as well as the chemist Antoine Lavoisier, a member of the commission.

80 the obvious reading of Genesis 38: Modern biblical scholarship tends to say Onan's crime was his failure to fulfill the obligation of levirate mar-riage, an ancient Hebrew custom that required a man to marry his broth-er's wife if the brother died without a male heir.

85 *call them all—Pandars!*: Obviously, not quite prescient enough. The term *pander* changed again post-Shakespeare. As a verb, *pander* went from meaning to act as a go-between for sex to a figurative use, associated espe-cially with politicians. That verb then produced a noun, *panderer*, with a different meaning from the original noun *pander*. Today the meaning of *pander* as "to pimp" exists only as a relic in U.S. legal code.

89 *paparazzi* has entered the world lexicon: In Japan, mothers who photo-graph their children's every move are called *mammarazzi*, a term making inroads in English as well.

91 statue of a warrior: The statue is thought to represent Menelaus (cuck-olded husband of Helen of Troy) carrying the body of Patroclus (Achilles' boon companion and boy toy).

96 a really silly fifties hairstyle: The coiffure, in a slightly different form, was first worn by La Pompadour and copied by men as well as women. The style had several variations but always involved sweeping the hair up off the face, and sometimes even fixing it to a wire frame.

96 Procrustes: In Greek, *Prokroustēs* literally means "the stretcher." The serial killer's real name, according to Apollodorus (the first known to write about him), was Damastes, though others have suggested the name Polypemon.

99 lacking the death penalty: Norway had not had a civilian execution since 1876, but capital punishment was still on the books for the military, where it remained until 1979.

101 when Nellie had a spell under the weather it was the one thing she could eat: Another story has it that the opera diva was on a diet and one day her thin dry toast arrived overdone, horrifying Escoffier, but Nellie wound up liking it that way. Melba, Dame'd in 1918, was born Helen Porter Mitchell; her stage name derives from her hometown of Melbourne, Australia.

101 Lemuel Benedict: His story, which he told the *New Yorker* in 1942, could well be a tall tale. There are many contenders to the plate. The original server of the dish may have been Delmonico's (with the name eggs à la Benedick), or perhaps a French provincial dish called *oeufs bénédictine* is the source of the recipe. Then again, maybe Delmonico's and French peasant cooks are a bunch of copycats.

102 (but no anchovies): Some say a salad with anchovies came first, whipped up by Cesare's brother Alex. However, others attribute the dish to chef Giacomo Junia of Chicago, who is said to have created it around 1903 and named it after Julius Caesar.

106 the crime of "moderatism": In a political sense, that is.

106 de Sade, by the way, was really fat: And short. But to be fair, it was only late in life that he "had eaten himself into a considerable, even a gro-tesque, obesity," as de Sade biographer Neil Schaeffer wrote in the *Guardian* in 2001.

106 Shrapnel: The meaning of the word extended from the shell to the projectiles it sent forth, and in that sense endured after the shell itself became obsolete technology. In Aussie and Kiwi military slang, *shrapnel* took on a further figurative meaning, of small bills or change.

109 burnsides; at some point the word did a flip-flop: The switch was probably influenced by "side-hair" and "side-whiskers," compound terms *sideburns* eventually replaced. Also popular in the U.S. was the word *dundrearies*, after the character Lord Dundreary in *Our American Cousin*, the play Lincoln attended the night he was shot.

115 a Renaissance man's Renaissance man: In the credit-where-credit-is-due department, I lifted this from Stephen Jay Gould's "a Renaissance man of the Renaissance itself," which is found in an excellent article on Fracastoro and syphilis Gould wrote for *Natural History* (Oct. 2000), and which is the source of most of my information on the subject.

115 blame it all on the French: Syphilis was widely called "the Spanish disease," but Fracastoro, for political reasons, hated the French and supported the Spanish, and so wanted to clear the latter's name and besmirch the former's.

117 stealing nectar and ambrosia: Alternate myths have it that Tantalus's crime was serving the gods human flesh at a banquet, or that he merely told his fellow mortals what the gossip was around the gods' dinner table.

125 "Money don't stink": What he actually said (reputedly) was *Pecunia non olet*, which became a standard Latin proverb.

127 "Jeep!": The original military vehicles were designated General Purpose, and so *jeep* may just be a clipped form of the initials G.P. Still, the popularity of Popeye, the identical spelling, and the fact that four-wheeled jeeps are magical and resourceful creatures themselves all indicate at the very least that Eugene exerted a Hooker-like influence on the name's popularity. (A similar argument can also be made with Wimpy/wimp, the connection between which is not universally accepted.)

128 blimp: The origin of the word *blimp* is unknown. The oft-cited etymology crediting it eponymously to Colonel Blimp is definitively apocryphal, the term having predated the cartoon character (who looks suspiciously like Count von Zeppelin).

130 *dummkopf*: Despite its flammability, hydrogen gives better lift than helium and was cheaper; in fact, it was the main gas used in airships before 1921.

131 *montgolfier* in French: Montgolfier was also once a word in English. Similar English-language fossils found in this essay are *roentgen rays* and *judas* in its peephole sense.

132 *Sprudelbad*: The most common term in German is *Whirlpool*, derived from English.

134 *bemelmans*, which means "foreigner who makes fun of natives": I was shocked when I came across travel writer Tom Miller's book *The Panama Hat Trail* and learned this about my grandfather. Miller quotes a Quito bookseller as saying that to carry *El Burro Por Dentro* would be suicidal, even forty years after its publication. To my relief, Miller also reported that certain people, intellectuals mostly, appreciated the book, claiming it spurred change and chalking the negative reception up to knee-jerk nationalism.

136 a couple of Englishmen and a kid who wrecked his father's wheels: The brougham was a four-wheel closed carriage, named after Scottish politician Henry Peter Brougham; the hansom a two-wheel closed carriage with the driver sitting at the back, designed by British architect Joseph Aloysius Hansom; and the phaeton a four-wheeled open carriage, named for the son of the sun god who ill-advisedly borrowed his father's chariot.

144 a macguffin: A macguffin is the gimmick around which a plot revolves but is in itself meaningless. According to Alfred Hitchcock, who coined the term, "In crook stories it is always the necklace and in spy stories it is always the papers."

A NOTE ON THE AUTHOR

JOHN BEMELMANS MARCIANO is the author and illustrator of several children's books, including *Madeline and the Cats of Rome*, *Harold's Tail*, and *Delilah*, as well as the illustrated biography *Bemelmans: The Life and Art of Madeline's Creator* about his grandfather Ludwig Bemelmans. An artist and self-professed word geek, he lives in Brooklyn with his wife, Andromache, daughter, Galatea, and two cats, Maud and Liddy.